Texas B

Hangouts

- 2nd Edition -

A Guide to Country Stores,
Backwoods Bars, and other
notable rural Texas venues
devoted to the relaxation,
comestation, and socialization arts.

by

Rich Houston & Heather Kuhn

ISBN:
ISBN- 13: 978-1500989682
ISBN-10: 1500989681

.

This book is dedicated to our families, especially the nieces and nephews: Coralie, Elise, Micaela, Braden, Ryan, Sarah, Cory, Isabelle, Ilsa, Chance, and Greer, as well as to all of the incredibly nice people we've met in our travels.

.

FORWARD

There was a lot of hard work put into making this book. It ain't easy drinking beer and eating barbecue and burgers under a shade tree in the country. Seriously, though, there has been a lot of miles driven and a lot of time spent researching and writing. We made sure and visited every place in this book, to insure that what we'd heard or read about was as good as it seemed.

Our goal was to include places that weren't well known- at least in the general public consciousness. There are a few exceptions, such as Luckenbach and Greune Hall, but leaving them out would have been too glaring an omission. Our guidelines for whom to include consisted of some of the following requirements: 1) they should be kind of far away, 2) they should have picnic tables under the trees, and 3) we would know it when we saw it. Obviously, we were pretty flexible with the first two requirements, since many of the places in the book aren't that far away and don't have shady picnic tables. What all the places had in common, though, was...well...I don't know what... but in France we call it *je ne sais quoi*. We knew it when we saw it and it just felt right.

Our goal was to make a guidebook that would be useful and unique not only to a family in the suburbs, but also to a jaded downtown hipster. Mostly, we just followed our noses- to sniff out places that we, ourselves, would like to go and hang out at. We did a lot of research, from old Texas Highways and Texas Monthly magazines, to the internets, and to just asking around. Many of these places we only found out about by asking other people if they knew of some cool backcountry place that they liked to hang out in. Several of them we were fortunate enough to discover just by driving past.

Of course, Texas is a big place and there are a lot of back roads yet to explore. We've tried to cover as many of them in Central Texas as we could for this first edition, but we're aiming for more. There's a lot of Texas still to see and we will be adding them to future editions. If you think you know of a place that we should see, please send us an email at: **tbchangouts@gmail.com**. In the meantime, we hope you will get out and visit some of these fantastic Texas gems. Each one has a unique character and charm. Each one is worth a drive through the beautiful Texas countryside. And each one (well, probably half of them at least) thinks that they have the best hamburger in Texas.*

While some of these places do good business, there are many which carry on only out of sheer orneriness, never making much money. It's up to us to support them, so as to keep alive the things we love best about Texas.

Rich Houston & Heather Kuhn
February 2014

* While many places had barbecue, even more had hamburgers- which are a bit less time and effort to cook up. Every one of them that we tried was delicious and it would be a difficult and futile endeavor to decide which was best. There's something about eating one outside in the country, with a cold beer, that just makes them all taste so darn good.

NOTES ON THE 2ND EDITION

Heather and I have felt incredibly blessed with all the support we've received over the past year since we first published Texas Backcountry Hangouts. Not only has the book sold pretty well, but we've also heard from many folks who told us how much they enjoyed using it to discover new places. Many people also like to comment on how many of the places they've been to and it seems that Alamo Springs, Hilltop Cafe, and Dry Creek Cafe are some of the most popular tourist attractions in Texas.

Since the first edition, we've been busy exploring new places. We've added several new Hangouts in the Hill Country, as well as more places north and east of Austin. Our goal is to cover the entirety of Texas, but it takes a long time to find these little hideouts and then go see them for ourselves. Texas is a big place and there are only so many weekends available for driving hundreds of miles. Nevertheless, we will continue to endeavour in our struggle to drink beer and eat delicious food, because we know that the people are counting on us.

In Memoriam-

Unfortunately, we lost a couple of Hangouts in the last year. The Big Horse Icehouse near Marble Falls fell victim to what we can only suppose was lack of business in its isolated area. Undoubtedly the continued low levels of nearby Lake Travis and the Colorado River didn't help. Up in Bend, on another part of the Colorado River, Spivey Barbecue decided to close its doors- although we've heard directly from the owner, Clay, that he really just got tired of doing it. Fortunately, Bad Bob's is still right next door and going strong with its peculiar blend of weirdness and dilapidated charm. The best that can be said about these closings is that at least they weren't any of the really historic places.

Maps and QR Codes-

In this 2nd edition, we've done away with the tiny not-very-specific maps next to each entry. At the request of several people, we've instead included a real map in the back of the book, which will hopefully give a better idea of where these places are- although you'll still need to consult a better map to find exact locations. Fortunately, we've included a pretty easy method of doing just that, right in the book. Next to each entry we've included a QR Code- which are those weird square barcode-looking thingies. QR Codes are pretty futuristic (or at least they were around 2006), but they are simple to use once you get to know them. To scan them, you'll need a smartphone with a QR Code Reader App. There are many available for free on any of the various Android, Apple, and Windows App Stores. Once you download the app, you can simply use the camera on your phone to scan the QR Code which should then automatically pull up a Google Map of the particular Backcountry Hangout you're searching for. (Never let it be said that Texas Backcountry Hangouts isn't interested in merging past and future by pushing the envelope and thinking outside of the box and using paradigm shifts to create disruptive synergy. Buzzword!)

And Finally-

Thanks again for taking a look at Texas Backcountry Hangouts and don't forget to drop us a line at **tbchangouts@gmail.com**. We would love to hear from you about any adventures you had or about a new place that we should take a look at.

Rich Houston & Heather Kuhn
November 2014

MUCH OBLIGED!

Special thanks to John Foster, Chris Tisdel, Shane Nowlin for all their support and help with editing, rewriting, navigation, and ideas. Also thanks to Wesley Lucas for the Sefcik tip.

CONTENTS

ALAMO SPRINGS

(830) 990-8004
www.alamospringscafe.com
107 Alamo Rd, Fredericksburg, TX 78624
Hours: 10:00am to 10:00pm, closed Tuesday.

Alamo Springs General Store and Cafe is not a country store, or a dancehall, or a bar. Still, it has some of the most important qualities in a backwoods attraction, which makes it worth including here. One of those qualities is that it's way the heck out in the middle of nowhere- southeast of Fredericksburg to be inexact. Another quality is that it has really really good food. If it was just an out of the way restaurant serving up mediocre fare, then Alamo Springs wouldn't be worth taking the time to visit. The food here, however, is known to be outstanding,-although we can't actually be sure of that, because all we could think of was trying the hamburgers, which have a far-flung reputation as being among the best. We just have to assume that if they do the rest of their extensive menu as well as their burgers- then it has to be good!

One of the things we liked about this place, besides the food, was the serve yourself coolers of beer and soda. The owners must assume that only the most trustworthy persons would make the long drive out here, because you just tell the cashier how many drinks you had when paying. It's that kind of informality and hospitality that makes Alamo Springs a great place in which to spend a few hours.

While Alamo Springs is primarily a restaurant, they also have a little bandstand out back- next to the picnic tables. They have live music playing every Friday and Saturday from 7pm-10pm.

One bonus of making the trek out to Alamo Springs is the Old Tunnel State Park, which is only about a hundred yards down the road from the restaurant. Formerly an old railroad tunnel- the park now hosts an enormous colony of bats, which one can view during summer evenings as they exit the tunnel. The walk down to the tunnel is very easy, making it a quick diversion- and the park also serves as good marker for where to turn, as the road to Alamo Springs isn't well labeled.

ALBERT ICE HOUSE

(830) 644-2042
www.alberttexas.com
5435 Ranch Road 1623, Stonewall, TX 78671

Situated southeast of Fredericksburg and a few miles south of Stonewall, the tiny town of Albert is hardly a town at all. More of a wide spot in the road would be a more accurate description. Still, what they've got there is more than worth seeing, especially if you're in the mood for a drive through some of the most beautiful Hill Country scenery around. Albert really just consists of the Albert Ice House, the Albert Dancehall, and an old schoolhouse that LBJ used to attend. Fortunately, they are all right next to each other and are filled to the brim with country gold.

The Albert Ice House, a comfortable, breezy bar, sits underneath two massive old oak trees. The old building has been renovated (but not too renovated) into a fantastic place to come hang out and have a few drinks. Inside you'll find the old wooden floor, a beautiful bar made from a single enormous tree trunk, open rafters, swing-up windows, a big screen TV, and comfortable high-backed bar chairs. Behind the bar you're likely to see Mike Haley- the very friendly bartender, who is also a fine Country musician in his own right. He can even officiate your wedding in the dancehall- if you're so inclined. For your drinking pleasure, the bar serves beer and wine, as well as the harder stuff.

Out in back of the Ice House is a large deck and patio, with plenty of picnic tables to relax on, underneath the deep shade of the oak trees. It's really just about as pleasant a spot as you could find- and it gets even better when you see that they have their very own food truck, called the Pig Pen. Food trucks are pretty rare in the Hill Country. Fortunately, Albert's food truck is run by the very capable Mike Moreno, who makes all the food himself from locally supplied meat and produce- there's no Sysco delivery here! The food, which includes delicious burgers, tacos, and more, makes excellent fare for a day spent playing horseshoes and drinking cold beer.

The Albert Dancehall sits just adjacent to the Ice House. It's a sprawling wooden-floored and corrugated tin-sided dancehall in the old Central Texas tradition. Occasionally open for dances, it's often rented out for weddings and private parties. If you ask nicely, Mike might let you take a look inside.

The biggest days at the Albert Ice House are Wednesday, Friday, and Saturday, when they have live music and the Pig Pen is open. Friday night at the Pig Pen is steak night, and the truck is also open on Sundays.

The Albert Ice House is a backwoods bar of the finest order. It's got the best qualities necessary for a top-notch hangout, including location, ambience, and a variety of colorful locals. Finally, if you're lucky enough to make it out there, be sure and sign the guest log- literally a wooden log- past ones of which are hung from the rafters above the bar.

ANDICE GENERAL STORE

(254) 793-3971
6500 FM 970, Georgetown, TX 78633

    The first thing you need to know about the Andice General Store is that it's clean. Really clean. The owner, Alan Thomas, is fanatical about getting a 100% rating from the Health Inspector, and he encourages good habits in his employees with healthy bonuses for a job well done. The second thing you need to know about this place is that they are serious about their hamburgers. It's obviously a major point of pride, as well as being a major draw, to have what is considered one of the best burgers in the state. They use fresh ingredients for all their burgers, sandwiches, and fries- and it shows!

Andice is a tiny burg, sitting about 45 minutes north of Austin, a few miles off of Highway 183, down FM 970. It's slightly larger and more happening than many of the old crossroads ranching communities that dotted Texas in the old days, but which have now largely died off as viable entities. Still, Andice is very small and the Andice General Store is the only place for many miles around to sell groceries, food, and drinks. Many of the old Country Stores have since converted over into being primarily restaurant/bars. Andice General Store, while not offering a wide range, nevertheless still has enough supplies to get a person by until they can run to HEB.

The store itself has been in existence for over a hundred years as a feed store and post office, as well as a general store. Mr. Thomas has owned it for a few years now and has done a lot of work fixing it up, without sacrificing the qualities that make it fun. The front of the building still looks like something out of the old west and there are picnic tables out to the side if you don't want to eat in the air-conditioning.

The Andice General Store is open 7 days a week, year round except for one week at Christmas. To go with the burgers, Andice has plenty of drinks, including old-timey sodas, as well as a good selection of beer for carry-out or drinking-in. At the counter, next to the jars of various pickled products (including the hitherto unknown pickled sausage), you're likely to find the owner's father, Sonny, taking orders and manning the register. He's about as friendly a guy as you're likely to run into and he's happy to tell you all about the history of the Andice Store and the area all around.

ANHALT HALL

(830) 438-2873
www.anhalthall.com
2390 Anhalt Road, Spring Branch, TX 78070

The Anhalt Dance Hall is one of those old German dance halls that dot the Texas countryside. The original hall was built in 1879 and the new modern addition to the hall has been in place since 1908. Roughly the size of a basketball court, Anhalt Dancehall serves up country, polka, and Cajun music roughly once a month.

Located north of San Antonio in Spring Branch, Anhalt Hall has the look of a particularly large and beat up metal barn. Its real charm, however, is inside with its polished wood dance floor and graceful arching rafters. Although not nationally known like Luckenbach, or even on the way to anywhere in particular, Anhalt Hall is a perfect stop for a traveler looking to make an authentic Texas Hill Country memory

Don't worry about bring a sack lunch either, they have a food and drink stand outside to wet your whistle and keep you going, in between dances.

BAD BOBS BEND STORE

(325) 628-3523
www.badbobsbendstore.com
112 CR 438, Bend, TX 76824
Hours: Monday thru Saturday 8:30pm to 6pm,
Sunday 9am to 5pm

Bad Bobs Bend Store is a great little place to check out- if your expectations aren't too high. Full of colorful characters and off the beaten path, Bad Bobs, located on the Colorado River in the tiny town of Bend, is somewhat like the general store in Oh Brother, Where Art Thou- they don't carry much and they're a geographical oddity- 2 weeks from everywhere.

Catering to a clientele of Bend locals and visitors to Colorado Bend State Park, Bad Bobs Bend Store has a product mix that seems to have been selected by and for men. Don't come here looking for feminine hygiene products or yogurt. Bad Bobs carries a fine assortment of chips, soda, beer, candy, bait, and, incongruously, vintage football and baseball trading cards. This is not 7-11… The off brand toilet paper and dried cat food comes from origins unknown. Bad Bobs also has a kitchen where you can order up some chow- like sandwiches or the legendary "Bad Burger".

The true charm of Bad Bobs Bend Store is evident on weekends when local musicians come to jam on the patio. Grabbing a cold beer from the cooler, and maybe a Bad Burger too, visitors are welcome to sit outside either on the front or back patios. The front patio has picnic tables and is a good place to watch the comings and goings of sleepy downtown Bend. The new back patio has a bandstand and plenty of seating- in fine country form, of course- around tables made from old wooden cable spools.

Bad Bobs Bend Store is really the only market around for miles and is located at the entrance road leading to both the magnificent Colorado Bend State Park and to a number of fishing camps located on the river. Spring through Fall is the time to visit, when the music is playing and a cold beer tastes best. Business reaches its peak in July when campers and fisherman are out in full force, and slows in the Fall. Bend is way too far from any major highway to attract the usual day-trippers. The characters there are real and strange and very friendly. This gives Bad Bobs that key ingredient in a country store which makes it worth a visit- authenticity.

BELMONT SOCIAL CLUB

(830) 424-3026
www.belmontsocialclubrestaurant.com
14395 U.S. 90 Alt, Gonzales, TX 78629

The Belmont Social Club Restaurant has seen a lot of history. In its time the hundred year old building has been modified, added to, and even moved on rollers. It's been an auto repair shop, a post office, a dentist office, a gas station, a restaurant, and a dancehall over the years. It's been in movies and it's played its part in the exploits of Bonnie and Clyde- the real ones, not the film version. Generations of locals have passed through its doors and they still stop by to have lunch, socialize, and reminisce.

Owned for most of its history by the Goss family, the Belmont Social Club was bought by Johnny Abrameit a few years ago and converted into a restaurant/dance hall. The big, old structure has a large kitchen where Johnny prepares lunch on weekdays. Lunch includes such items as catfish and barbeque sandwiches, which are some of the best we've ever tried. On weekends the Belmont hosts bands and dances which are open to the whole family. For drinks they have beer and wine and, of course, sweet tea.

Located in the middle of the semi-ghost town of Belmont, south of Luling, the Belmont Social Club Restaurant is pretty far from any populated area. On weekdays, though, there are friendly locals always stopping by to eat and chat, and on weekends, the place fills up with people from all around the neighboring towns. It's a great country place to make a destination, or to just stop by for a delicious meal and good conversation. With all the history of the place, there are plenty of stories to hear and good times to be had.

BLUFF DALE

The Greenwood: (254) 728-3735
Let's Eat: (254) 728-3635

The town of Bluff Dale is tiny- but they seem able to squeeze a lot of backcountry goodness into this little place. Situated on Highway 377, between Stephenville and Granbury, Bluff Dale has three great places to hang out at.

The Greenwood Saloon in Bluff Dale is your garden variety Texas hangout. Catering mostly to bikers, it's a pretty cool place to come and take a load off while sipping a cold beer. Stuffed full of taxidermy and old furniture, the old one-room building could almost double as an antique store, if not for the crowd of noisy revelers inside.

The Greenwood is situated at the end of a strip of old "downtown" buildings on Greenwood Street, next to the railroad tracks. Down the street is Wilfong's Cajun Shack and Oyster Bar. Built, owned, and operated by Stephanie Wilfong, the place has a nice open-air patio surrounded by palms- to give it that island vibe. (Wilfong's is not the only business Stephanie owns. She's also got a deer processing shop next door, which has an almost all-girl crew of butchers.)

Right across the street from Wilfong's is the hole-in-the-wall haute-cuisine restaurant called "Let's Eat". Housed in the old, extremely bland looking, former post office, Let's Eat is a dazzling urban find in such a rustic setting.

Let's Eat features a seasonal menu based on locally sourced products. The two other things you need to know is that it's BYOB and it helps to make a reservation- as it fills up almost every night.

While the Greenwood is the only place in Bluff Dale that would stand alone as a formal "Texas Backcountry Hangout", the conglomeration of these three cool bars/restaurants in such a small locale makes for an inviting triple-threat that we couldn't pass up. Bluff Dale may be way out in the middle of nowhere, but it's definitely worth the trip.

CASTELL GENERAL STORE

(325) 247-4100
19522 W Ranch Rd 152, Llano, TX 78643

The Castell General Store does everything right when it comes to a backcountry hangout. Everything here seems designed to make a body forget the outside world. Situated in the middle of the tiny community of Castell- 20 miles west of Llano next to the Llano river, the Castell General Store is a combination bar, barbeque joint, convenience store, and bait shop. On any given weekend, you can find a combination of locals and tourists hanging out on the porch or socializing at the picnic tables under the big old oak tree, eating barbeque and drinking beer. Ask nicely and you might get something stronger from one of the regulars- it's often Big Red and Vodka, heavy on the vodka.

On weekends, it's not uncommon to have a group of musicians outside desultorily picking the banjo or playing guitar. Inside, in the air-conditioning, you can sit at the bar or tables and watch the game- whatever sport is in season. There's no schedule and , once you get here, there's no real hurry to do anything or go anywhere else.

The Castell General Store is situated about 100 yards from the beautiful Llano river. Lots of folks take advantage of the proximity to walk down and jump in when it gets hot out. For those feeling more adventurous, kayak rentals are also available at the store. The unspoiled and largely undeveloped Llano River makes for a tranquil and beautiful ride.

On weekend days, the Castell Store always has barbecue on the pit. The mesquite-wood coals make for some perfectly cooked and juicy brisket or sausage. To get some, just go to the pit and have them cut some off for you, then head inside to pay and to get a drink. After 5pm, the owner Mark cooks up one of the best burgers in the Hill Country- which is saying a lot, since most country stores claim to have the best burgers. Mark doesn't make any claims and doesn't need to. The burgers speak for themselves.

Castell was the earliest town built by the German settlers in the Llano area. However, despite being in an old building, the Castell General Store doesn't have any sort of grand history to it. It's not the oldest or most historic or the most lauded country store in Texas- but it's probably the best. It has the type of atmosphere and style by which all other country stores should be measured. There's nothing precious or sentimental about its charms. It's simply the perfect place to relax and have a good time without any pretentions.

Notable events at the Castell General Store include the annual Goat Cook-off, Testicle Festival (cattle and turkey testicles fried up and delicious), and WesFest (celebrating the birthday of a notable louche patron).

CELE STORE

(512) 869-9340
www.celestore.com
18726 Cameron Road, Manor, TX 78653

The Cele Store looks like an old barn in a state of extreme disrepair. It's last paintjob was probably in 1950. The store is situated at a little country crossroads with not much else around it. If you didn't know better, you might even think it's abandoned. Despite its looks, though, the Cele Store is the place to be if you're interested in really good things like: barbecue, live country music, beer, and friendly folks.

Like a lot of these country places, the Cele Store (pronounced like "seal") got its start in the late 1800's as a saloon and later became a general store, post office, and community center. Over the years, it's been added on to and "decorated" in traditional backwoods style- which only adds to the charm. Step inside and you'll see the original bar, which was brought over from Germany in the 1800's. The rest of the decor could be described as Rural Opportunistic Style. It's eclectic and has been pulled together from wherever it could be found.

The Cele Store serves great barbecue, cooked to perfection on their brick pit, which was built in 1964. It's the pit which gives the barbecue it's taste-having been seasoned down the decades. Oddly enough, though- you have to bring your own sides, as the only vegetables they offer are pickles and onions.

Movie producers seem to love the Cele Store- probably because it just looks so darn authentic. Over the years, it's been featured in films such as: Secondhand Lions, A Perfect World, and the Texas Chainsaw Massacre. The country location of the Cele Store might not last, though. In a few years, it might just be surrounded by the suburbs that are creeping out from north Austin. What used to be a tiny crossroads farming and ranching village is now almost within sight of suburban sprawl.

The Cele Store is only open Thursday through Saturday. Thursday they serve dinner only, Fridays they serve both lunch and dinner, and Saturdays they serve lunch only. Reservations are recommended, but they never turn anyone away if you show up unannounced- you just might have to wait a while. On Fridays they have a band and the tiny dance floor is open to all. It's a good time for the whole family at this iconic Texas locale.

CIRCLEVILLE STORE

512-352-6848
www.circlevillestore.com
600 S State Highway 95, Taylor, Texas

Sitting a few miles north of Taylor on Highway 95, the Circleville Store ain't pretty. Something of a Frankenstein's monster of a building, the place has been around for more than 80 years and is located in the tiny no-stoplight community of Circleville. Fortunately, the surrounding farms, particularly by the nearby San Gabriel river, are as picturesque as can be. The drive from Georgetown, east on Highway 29, is a very scenic little journey down through the bottomland farms of the area.

What used to be a more comprehensive store and gas station is now mostly a country restaurant and entertainment venue. Inside the large store, you can sit and chow down on some classic country fare, such as mouthwatering burgers, steaks, and fried chicken. Being off of the tourist circuit, the Circleville Store has a decidedly local feel to it, with ranchers, farmers, and families coming in to socialize and have a bite to eat. It's not exclusionary, though. Owners Joe and Nikki Barcuch are as friendly and welcoming to outsiders as can be.

In addition to the restaurant portion of the store, there's now a new live music venue out back. What was once an old storage building has been converted into a large stage, welcoming some top-notch country acts on warm weekends. Just to keep it legit, there's also a bait shop directly next to the stage- in case you feel inspired to do a little fishing between sets.

However you get there, the Circleville Store is a great little place to get away to- with cold beer and good food served out the back of the store while you listen to some great music on a warm Texas evening.

CISTERN COUNTRY STORE

(361) 865-3655
www.cisternstore-bar.com
12604 Texas 95, Flatonia, TX 78941

The Cistern Country Store sits way out amid the farmlands east of Austin, on Highway 95, between Flatonia and Smithville. A fairly nondescript little building, it's something of a personality test when you pull up to this place and are confronted with a choice of two doors- one labeled "store" and other labeled "bar". Fortunately, once inside you see that the choice is not so stark. Both the bar and the store are connected and pretty permeable. On the store side you have a neat little deli, serving up both hot and cold food, as well as selling the basic necessities of life for this isolated location. There are a couple of nice tables ,with gingham tablecloths, to sit at or you can take it to the other side and eat at the bar.

The bar side of the Cistern Country Store is as functional and cozy as the store side. Nevertheless, it contains everything one might want in a country bar, including the plywood-floored dance floor, bandstand, a couple of pool tables, and jukebox. One can tell, from the graffiti laden walls, that this place has been around for a long time. More than a hundred years, according to the local lore.

Friday and Saturday at the Cistern they often have live music or karaoke and the place fills up with locals, as well as those traveling around enjoying the pretty farmland scenery of the area. There may not be much to the town of Cistern, but there's a lot to love about the Cistern Country Store.

CISTERN SCHOOL HOUSE

(361) 865-1500
9703 Fm 2237, Flatonia, TX 78941

When we were checking out the Cistern Country Store, we were told that there was another place in town that we might want to visit as well. Not expecting that a tiny town the size of Cistern could support much more in the way of bars, we approached the Cistern Schoolhouse with some trepidation. The place is just a couple of hundred yards from the Cistern Country Store, down county road 2237. Looking way more like the old schoolhouse that it used to be, than the bar it now is, the Cistern Schoolhouse is non-descript and completely lacking in signage- other than an old rusted school bus that sits out front by the road.

Once inside though, we were completely surprised by how inviting the place was. Restored to it's original style, the four room building now has a large bar in one room, and another large (class)room dedicated solely to pool tables, shuffleboard, and other games.

Owned and operated by Sue and Daniel Kalinec, the building was actually used as a schoolhouse until 1974. The Kalinec's opened it up in its current incarnation in 2005. The wood interior has a warm and comfortable feel to it, and the Kalinec's have done a good job of restoring it to its original luster. The building itself has an interesting history, dating back to when it was built in 1941- which the Kalinec's will be happy to tell you all about.

The Cistern Schoolhouse is open every day but Tuesday and Wednesday.

On Fridays there's usually a group of musicians that come to jam, but the session is open to everyone. Thursdays are Free Game Night- but shuffleboard is always free. While you're in there, check out the amazing assortment of beers, which is comparable to that of a good bar in any big city. For those not into beer, they also have wine and wine spritzers available, as well as setups.

While not necessarily a destination in and of itself, the Cistern Schoolhouse Bar definitely makes a pleasant and unique little stop if you're passing by.

CRIDER'S RODEO

(830) 238-4441
www.cridersrodeoanddance.com
8314 Texas 39, Hunt, TX 78024

Ninety years. That's how long Crider's Rodeo and Dancehall has been serving up a Hill Country mix of cowboy fun. It takes dedication to continue that type of business for almost a century. Then again, it's not hard to see why the Crider family keeps it going- they're only open during the summer and they're doing two things Texan's love to do- rodeo-ing and partying. What's not to like?

Crider's is located way back in the hinterlands of Hunt, along the banks of the Guadalupe River. If you find your way to Kerrville, then head west to Ingram, and then south along the Cypress-lined river to Hunt- and then keep going- you'll eventually get to Crider's Rodeo. The grounds contain a beat-up, but completely functional, rodeo arena, a good-sized dirt parking lot, an outdoor cement dance-floor and stage, and a large country bar. Don't let the rustic description dissuade you from coming though. The whole is greater than the sum of its parts. Crider's Rodeo and Dancehall is a well lived in place.

Start with the rodeo. What could be finer than a summer evening watching the Texas national sport? Maybe it's not the biggest or the best, but it's got that small-town soul. Afterwards, a short walk will take you to the bar where you can cool off with a cold beer and maybe get some grub while you wait for the dance to start. There's a good jukebox, pool tables, and plenty of tables. When the dance gets going, you can two-step around the big old Live Oak tree in the middle of the dancefloor or just sit at a picnic table and enjoy the band.

Crider's is open every weekend during the summer, with a rodeo and dance on both Friday and Saturday nights. While the riverfront properties surrounding it might be now in the seven-figure range, and the neighbors might include a few Hollywood celebrities, Crider's still retains the charm it had when it opened in 1925, when it was really an isolated outpost.

CROSSROAD TAVERN AT CAT SPRING

(979) 357-4808
1216 FM 1094 Rd, Cat Spring, TX 78933

The Crossroad Tavern is about as old-school as you can get. Opened in 1952, It's a vintage cross-roads gas station and diner that still functions as both- without having to resort to any modern tricks like selling art-glass or shamelessly playing up its nostalgia quotient. It's a neatly kept, airy, white-painted, old-fashioned service station of the sort that used to dot the countryside from coast to coast- in the days before interstates and Buccees-style mega-stations. While you won't be able to stop and get a lube job or change your spark plugs, you can still fill up and grab a cold road-soda to enjoy as you explore the lovely scenic hills of the area.

The Crossroad Tavern is located just north of a little burg with the lyrical name of Cat Spring, at the crossing of Highways 949 and 1094, about 11 miles northwest of Sealy. Inside you'll find a lunch counter, serving up basic burgers and sandwiches for lunch, as well as roast beef and pork roasts on Monday and Tuesday. The small store sells necessities like white bread and paper towels. Out front there are some comfortable shaded benches where you can drink a beer and watch the laconic traffic of this isolated area.

Despite its name, the Crossroad Tavern isn't a beer joint. Owners Bonnie and William Hegemeyer have run the place for 27 years- just like Bonnie's parents did for 25 years before that. Also, despite the sign on the front of the building that says 'Cat Spring Country Club', the Crossroad Tavern isn't a club either. (The sign was put up as a joke by a regular.) It's more of a community gathering spot that happens to serve beer and wine. The Hegemeyers don't let it get rowdy or let the language get too salty, and the local farmers and ranchers who gather here in the afternoons mostly just discuss the weather or cattle prices.

The Crossroad Tavern is open from about 6am to 8pm most days. On Fridays and Saturdays, they close at 11pm, and they are closed on Sundays. Friday evenings are the time to come if you want to experience the real community feeling of the place, when they serve up an all-you-can-eat Fish Fry. For $10 you can get a full meal with all the fixins' and a drink. It's a family affair, with plenty of folks sitting on the side patio while the kids run around and tire themselves out.

While it doesn't have an old dancehall or an outsized reputation, the Crossroad Tavern still has all it needs to be a great country hangout. It's a real place with real people.

DAHLIA'S CAFE

(512) 515-7772
www.dahliacafe.com
2450 RR 1869, Liberty Hill, TX 78642
Hours: Tuesday thru Saturday 7am to 9pm

The place seems small at first approach, but as you drive around out back to a large parking lot and walk into the frenetic atmosphere, you realize this place does swift business- and you soon see why. On a Saturday night there was a 40 minute wait for a table for 5, and the wait was worth every minute.

After parking out back you walk up to a large outdoor area with a fantastic old-school kids playground, several pits for playing Washers, a bar that doubles as a stage for live music when the weather permits, and several picnic tables and other seating. Even on chilly nights, there are kids running around and adults waiting for tables, beers in hand. The atmosphere is very casual and comfortable.

Once inside several young and friendly hostesses are on hand to take your name, and there is a seating area with ample room while you wait. That same room was previously a deck, but is now covered and fronted with large roll-up doors that open up in good weather for al fresco dining, rain or shine. The inside dining room has a bare bones décor, including a ceiling that is sound insulated with hundreds of egg cartons.

The lunch and dinner menus are full of comfort food – chicken fried chicken or steak, burgers, chicken-and-waffle sliders, meat loaf and sandwiches as well as salads and soups. There are a ton of sides to pair with your entree such as fried okra, sautéed spinach, mashed potatoes and mac-and-cheese. Breakfast offerings include such delicious and non-calorie friendly pancakes, waffles, migas, and plenty of combo plates, including the "God Bless Texas". The day staff tends to be seasoned waitresses that remember you by name and call you honey or sweetie.

Everything is absolutely delicious, and the fried chicken is definitely some of the best around. Dahlia's is family friendly, fun and worth a trip to Liberty Hill. It's a country restaurant with a down home style.

DRY CREEK CAFE AND BOAT DOCK

(512) 453-9244
4812 Mt Bonnell Rd, Austin, TX 78731

It might seem strange to include the Dry Creek Cafe and Boat Dock in a list of country stores and backwoods bars, namely because Dry Creek is within the Austin city limits and is a fairly short drive away from downtown. Once you've been there, though, you'll understand.

Sitting on Mt. Bonnell road, the Dry Creek Cafe and Boat Dock is neither a cafe nor a boat dock. It's a backwoods dive bar at its finest. It's a remnant of a time long past, when the area out by Mt. Bonnell wasn't almost exclusively populated by the 1%, but was rather a country lane on the way to the lake, popular with redneck fishermen and the local drinking gentry.

The old beat-up two story building houses one bar downstairs- manned by some characters who clearly haven't gotten the memo about the new sense of decorum in the area. There's a pool table in back and a jukebox playing old country on scratchy speakers. Upstairs is a deck overlooking the trees and hills near the lake. That's pretty much it- and it's perfect.

They sell beer only and you have to bring your bottle back before you can get another one. Helps with cleanup, you know. The hours of Dry Creek vary, but they don't stay open too late. 4pm until 9ish, is about normal. The whole thing has the feel of going over to a friends grandparents old lake house. The vibe is relaxed and nobody is worried about how they look. It's pure country, right in the middle of town.

DUTCHMAN'S HIDDEN VALLEY

(254) 386-3018
www.dutchmans-hiddenvalley.com
281 Hamilton Dr, Hamilton, TX 76531

Dutchman's Hidden Valley is a country store on steroids. Located a few miles north of Hamilton on Highway 281, Dutchman's Hidden Valley has just about anything a traveler could desire. Start with the food. Not content to merely serve up delicious food, Dutchman's makes many items from scratch- including breads, smoked sausage and cheese, and candies. After that, Dutchman's can sell you everything from gardening supplies to antiques to toys to beauty products. The sprawling 10 room store (made from old Air Force barracks) has something for everyone and it's hard not to spend an hour just wandering around.

The heart of Dutchman's Hidden Valley is the kitchen. They serve up a variety of deli sandwiches, sausages, and desserts, which can be taken to go or eaten in their cozy dining room. When it's cool out, sitting by the fireplace is a real delight. Elsewhere, scattered variously about the rambling place, you'll find such devices as a pecan sheller, a peanut roaster, a mechanical pepper grinder, and a long marble table where they make all of their own fudge and other candies. There's also so many varieties of pickled and canned goods, that they have had to squeeze them in at various spots around the store, to be able to display them all.

Dutchman's Hidden Valley isn't the type of place you're going to go to and hang out with a beer and a band for a few hours. It's more like a roadside attraction, than your typical backcountry hangout. Still, it's a country store that is a delight for the senses and a welcome respite during a long drive. If you're driving on 281 and want to stop at a place where you can stretch your legs, grab lunch and a souvenir, at a place the whole family can enjoy, then Dutchman's is the spot for you.

FLOORE COUNTRY STORE

(210) 695-8827
www.liveatfloores.com
14492 Old Bandera Rd., Helotes, TX 78023

The Floore Country Store is the quintessential Texas honky-tonk. Never mind the fact that the encroaching suburbs of San Antonio threaten its status as a legitimate country store. It's not exactly offering much for sale to local ranchers. What it does offer is an atmosphere and flavor that stands with the best Texas dancehalls. On practically any weekend night, you can see great country music on either their indoor or outdoor stages. The Floore Store gets some of the best too. Over the years it's hosted such notables as Merle Haggard, Bob Dylan, Elvis, and many, many more.

The Floore Country Store has been in existence for over 60 years. Located in the small town of Helotes, just outside of San Antonio, you can't miss the place- what with all the signs it has out front. Inside is a nice big bar, serving both beer and wine, as well as booze. They also serve food, which can be eaten at the tables surrounding the dance floor. On the menu is a wide selection of the usual Texas foods like chicken-fried steak, barbecue, and catfish.

This is the kind of place that musicians love to play in, with its rafters full of hanging boots, painted signs warning of fines for fighting, or it's fireplace for cold nights. It's also the kind of place that has everything you could ask for in a dancehall. Make no mistake, the Floore Country Store is as good as it gets when it comes to pure honky-tonk legitimacy. It's no wonder that Texas Monthly listed going to the Floore Country Store as one of the "50 Things Every Texan Should Do".

FREIHEIT COUNTRY STORE

(830) 625-9400
www.freiheitcountrystore.net
2157 Fm 1101, New Braunfels, TX 78130

The Freiheit Country Store is a relic of times past. At least times past for New Braunfels. Back in the old days, folks would drive out in the country to the Freiheit Store to get some delicious dinner and listen to some good music. They'd come for the burgers, fries, and onion rings, as well as the wiener-schnitzel and chicken-fried steak. Out back they would drink and dance in the open air dancehall, amid the fields and back roads.

Fortunately, most of that still exists. All except for the driving out in the country part. It's only a matter of a couple of years until the Freiheit Country Store is surrounded by the unstoppable flood of commercial development. Freiheit isn't far from I-35, and the corridor between Austin and San Antonio is hot property. Already there are office buildings nearby. Will the Freiheit Country Store survive? Probably. It's too good and too beloved to get rid of, merely for the sake of putting up another strip mall. Will it lose some of its charm? Maybe. Still, it will exist as a living relic and reminder of what we all love about Texas.

FRONTIER OUTPOST

(830) 997-0099
9821 Ranch Road 965, Fredericksburg, TX 78624

If you've ever driven ranch road 965, which runs between Fredericksburg and Enchanted Rock, then you've probably driven by the Frontier Outpost. Evoking the style of an old west storefront, the Frontier Outpost harkens back to a day when the area around was as remote a location as one could find in Central Texas- when it could take a day or more to reach Fredericksburg or Llano. Fortunately, these days it's a bit easier to reach the Frontier Outpost, but it still feels like a lost corner of civilization, tucked back among the dry hills and cedar trees.

The Frontier Outpost was built way back in aught-eight (of this century). Owner John Hardaway constructed the rough building himself, with an eye towards giving it an old and dusty look. He's succeeded brilliantly, as the place looks like it's been there for a hundred years already- with it's faded wood false front and tin covered porch. Inside, the tin walls, pot-bellied stove, and shelves of supplies enhance the forlorn general store theme. The main reasons most people stop by though, are lined up behind the bar- bottles of beer. The Frontier Outpost is a right-fine place to stop by and sip a cold one after a hard day spent working on the ranch, or more likely, hiking the trails or rock-climbing at Enchanted Rock.

The Frontier Outpost has supplies geared towards the day-tripper or overnight camper. There's stuff like sunblock, cans of beans, hotdogs, sodas, and marshmallows. In addition to the store, there's also a campground out to the side of the place, where prices are an affordable $5 a person. Many folks prefer to stay here, rather than deal with the rules and regulations of the campgrounds at Enchanted Rock. Not only is it a less formal atmosphere, but on weekends there is entertainment to be had for campers and visitors alike.

Every Friday and Saturday evening the Frontier Outpost has live music out back on the deck. John, the owner, often plays with his band 30.06 (Thirty-aught-six) and other musicians often drop by as well. You can get a beer and sit out in the country air while listening to the music, or you can bring your own liquor- although booze is encouraged to be shared with the band. There's some barbecue pits out to the side too, if you feel like cooking up some food. Any way you do it, the Frontier Outpost is a great little place to stop in and kill some time in the heart of the Hill Country.

GARVEN STORE

(830) 640-3235
www.garvenstore.com
27304 N. Highway 83, Mountain Home, TX 78058
Hours: Monday thru Saturday 8am to 7pm,
Sunday 9:30am thru 6pm

The little crossroads gas station called Garven Store is just about as far from anywhere as a person would want to be. Situated at the crossroads of Highways 41 and 83, about 40 miles west of Kerrville, Garven store sits in singular isolation. Having the distinction of being one of the oldest convenience stores is Texas might sound like a dubious honor, but Garven Store provides a glimpse back in time to the early days of auto travel. Small anachronisms like the pressed tin ceiling, old(ish) style gas pumps, above ground gas storage tanks, and the classic gas station building design, all harken back to a time before interstates, truck stops and fast food restaurants.

Garven Store isn't just about nostalgia, though. Inside, a country roads traveler can find one of the best selections of beef jerky in Texas. Homemade by the owners, they have about a dozen different types of delicious jerky to choose from. Also inside is a large selection of Garven Store brand pickled products- from quail eggs to pickled carrots to everything in between. If that isn't enough, you can grab a drink and one of their excellent barbecue sandwiches and enjoy yourself in their outdoor dining area.

And, if you're thinking, "How am I going to divide up my dried meats and pickled products like a country traveler?"...Well, Garven Store has you covered there too. This final item for your trip is available next to the cash register- three large boxes of knives are available to pick through and purchase for $5 apiece.

While most people won't seek out Garven Store for all of its "pretty", you will leave knowing that you found an interesting nexus at the crossroads of past and present. One could spend an hour just looking at all the details on the building itself, cobbled together over a period of 70 plus years. One could also admire the pet peacock which spends its time strutting around and which is apparently used as a "guard-peacock". The best thing to do there, however, is just talk to the locals- who can tell some of the craziest and most amazing stories that a traveler may ever hear... and in Texas, that's sayin' somethin'!.

GREEN FLY BBQ AND COUNTRY STORE

(512) 756-4580
10425 Highway 281 North (Lake Victor Turnoff),
Burnet, TX 78611

The Green Fly Barbecue and Country Store, like all truly good country stores, seems to sit at the intersection of nowhere and out-of-the-way. Located on Highway 281, between Lampasas and Burnet, the Green Fly isn't on most of the usual tourist circuits. Talk to the owners, though, and you'll soon learn that 281 has become a significant alternative route for those wishing to avoid the headaches of I-35. Taking care of travelers and locals, alike, the Green Fly does brisk business with its unique combination barbecue restaurant and eclectic boutique.

Housed in an almost century-old former gas station/store, the Green Fly Barbecue and Country Store has been open for business since May of 2013. Started by Nikki and Brett Coughran as a sort of retirement project, the Green Fly serves up delicious barbecue every day of the week, except Mondays and Tuesdays. Owner/Cook Brett Coughran cooks up some tasty brisket, just the way he likes it- tender, juicy, and falling apart. In addition to the brisket, they offer ribs, sausage and turkey. One of the distinguishing features of the place, though, is the variety of sides and desserts available, including such items as Jalapeno-Cilantro Slaw, Corn Casserole, and even an unheard of Chocolate Cobbler! To wash it down there's the usual iced tea, but also an unusually large selection of old-fashioned Dublin sodas.

On the country store side of the building, Nikki Coughran offers up a dizzying array of tchotchkes, from lawn art to Green Fly-brand pickled foods to jewelry and more. Also owning 'The Boutique' on the square in Llano, Nikki knows a thing or two about what people like, and it's hard not to find something at the Green Fly that you realize you can't do without.

While the Green Fly isn't on the way to most Hill Country weekend destinations, it still makes a good end-point for what is a really scenic country drive. The back roads between 281 and Bertram are full of great bucolic scenery, especially during the Spring-time. After traveling through the prairies and woodlands north of Bertram, the Green Fly Barbecue and Country Store makes for a great lunch break stop. With its distinctive green signs and giant metal giraffe out front, you can't miss it- and there's plenty of room to sit inside in the A/C or outside on the picnic tables and rocking chairs on the porch.

GRUENE HALL

(830) 606-1281
gruenehall.com
1281 Gruene Rd, New Braunfels, TX 78130

Gruene Hall is probably the best known of the old Texas dancehalls. Founded in 1878, Gruene Hall (pronounced "Green"), has been continuously operating since that time. The building looks like it hasn't been renovated since then either- and that's pretty darn cool. Inside the old wooden building, there's a bar in front and the dancehall in back. The wooden floors are buckled and worn smooth from generations of dancers, and the walls still display the old advertisements. The stage, which features an old-time mural on the back wall, has hosted pretty much all of the Texas musical greats- too numerous to even begin to list. Off to the side, there's a huge outdoor area, which is just about as perfect a place to relax and drink a cold beer as a person could ask for on a warm summer night.

Sitting in a position very similar to the Freiheit Store on the other side of I-35, Gruene Hall is basically surrounded by suburbs. Fortunately, Gruene Hall seems to be slightly better positioned to survive- as there is a strong desire from both the businesses in Gruene, which thrive on the tourism, and the citizenry of the suburbs themselves to keep Gruene alive. While hardly "back-country" anymore, Gruene Hall and the tiny town of Gruene still retain the rustic charm which has made it an international icon.

HARRY'S ON THE LOOP

(512) 919-9130
2732 RR 1323, Willow City, TX 78675
Hours: Friday 12pm to 12am, Saturday 12pm to 1am,
Sun 12pm to 6pm

Located on the Willow City Loop in Willow City, Harry's had for years been a well known watering hole. It had fallen into decline and closure over the past few years until the current owners, Shawn Graf and Carla Gerlich, bought it and set about revitalizing the place. And by revitalizing- we mean that they've opened it, put out some picnic tables, and settled in to wait for people to once again discover this little gem of a hangout. It's the type of place that trying to "fix up" would ruin its character. From the parking lot with its hundreds of thousands of flattened bottle caps to the wood burning stove in the middle of the room to the half wild backyard-Harry's is the real deal.

What Harry's lacks in amenities is more than made up for in history and character. The proprietor is full of stories and factoids about the establishment, the area, and the local characters that will leave you reeling, laughing, and feeling a tad disbelieving if he were not so sincere and open. Stories of local witches, hauntings (of Harry's bar itself), secret military bases, and cowboy & indian lore all get mixed together at Harry's.

On weekends at Harry's there's often some barbecue cooking, and you can throw a few washers out back. Bring your hog or your rod or just your bicycle. Any way you get there, it's a perfect spot to relax for a few hours with a cold one in the heart of the Hill Country.

HEADWATERS SALOON

(830) 864-4055
www.headwaterssaloon.com
229 South Ranch Road 783, Harper, Texas 78631
Hours: Open 7 days a week at noon

If you happen to find yourself in Harper, Texas- and there's usually little reason to be there, other than passing through- then you should take some time and check out the Headwaters Saloon. Harper is a small town 22 miles west of Fredericksburg. Before, when most of the counties to the north and west were dry counties which didn't allow the sale of alcoholic beverages, Harper had 7 bars in town- which catered to both locals and thirsty out-of-towners. A few years ago, the number of bars had dwindled to zero. As one regular at the Saloon put it- Harper used to have 7 bars and 7 churches- and the churches won. The Headwaters Saloon, which opened in 2012, has ameliorated the situation by providing a nice, family-friendly venue tucked away just south of town on Hwy 783.

The Headwaters Saloon gets its name from the fact that it's located near the headwaters of the Pedernales River, which at that spot is nothing more than a small seasonal creek. Owned and operated by Vic and Lori Hollender, the Headwaters includes not only a nice bar, dancefloor, bandstand, and outdoor area- but also several cabins for rent. It would be a stretch to say that the cabins are anywhere near luxurious, but they provide a nice little spot to stay in if you're planning on staying and listening to the band or if you just need a place to rest your head during your back roads explorations.

If you want to plan an even bigger weekend, the Hollenders have also built a large pavilion close to the bar, which can be used for events like a family reunion or your biker rally. Additionally, plans are in the works for an RV Park, too. One great event that they've got going on at the Headwaters Pavilion is the "Headwaters for Heroes" which helps out combat veterans and provides them with hunting and fishing trips.

The folks at Headwaters are real nice and they're biker friendly. While the Saloon is open every day, weekends are the most popular- with bands playing on Saturday nights. For drinks, they've got beer and wine coolers and outside the dancefloor, with its large roll-up door, there is a fire pit and picnic tables. So swing on by and relax with some of the nicest folks in the Hill Country.

HILLTOP CAFE

(830) 997-8922
www.hilltopcafe.com
10661 N US Highway 87, Fredericksburg, TX 78624
Hours: Tuesday through Sunday for Lunch and Dinner

The Hilltop Cafe defies expectations. If you're expecting some mediocre chicken fried steak and hamburger joint, then you're going to be pleasantly surprised. Not content to merely serve traditional fare, the Hilltop Cafe offers up delicious Mediterranean and Cajun cuisine as well. The mix isn't accidental either. This family owned restaurant has been in operation since 1980 and is run by Johnny and Brenda Nicholas, their son Willie, and a couple of Aunts too. Johnny has a Greek heritage and Brenda, who grew up in Fredericksburg, got the Cajun influence from time spent in Port Arthur.

Located in an old-style converted gas station, the Hilltop is an oasis among the ranches west of Fredericksburg. The neon sign in the distance proclaiming "Beer" welcomes you inside the comfortable old rambling building, filled with eclectic décor celebrating music, food, travel, and Texas culture.

The menu at the Hilltop is decidedly upscale and eclectic for a location so remote. You'll find everything from crab cakes to escargot, flaming Greek cheese to Oysters Bruton, and pork chops to fried catfish. Still, the friendly down-home service in this family run restaurant is as far away from cosmopolitan snobbery as you can get.

Not only is cooking a family tradition, but so is music. Johnny Nicholas has played in many bands and with many musicians, most notably Asleep at the Wheel and the Fabulous Thunderbirds. Johnny still plays many weekend nights at the Hilltop, along with other guests who stop by. Setting up right there in the dining room, it's a complete entertainment experience with the delicious food, friendly atmosphere, and some good music.

The Hilltop Cafe isn't on the way to anything in particular. Located on Highway 87, it's 10 miles outside of Fredericksburg, going northwest on the way to Mason. It's a bit of a hike to get there, but it's so good that on weekend nights it's always packed. So, make your reservation and go have some of the best non-country backcountry cuisine in Texas.

HORNY TOAD BAR AND GRILL

(254) 597-1100
www.hornytoadbar.com
319 North 3rd Street, Cranfills Gap, TX 76637

③

The Horny Toad Bar and Grill is a youngster in the Backcountry Hangouts scene, only having opened in 2006. Still, the old converted tin warehouse that houses the joint has enough of the patina of age to make up for the youth of this upstart. It doesn't hurt that the Horny Toad is located in not-so-bustling downtown Cranfills Gap- an out of the way micropolis north-west of Waco that has seen more prosperous days. The pride of the Norwegians who originally settled here can be seen in the relative neatness of the town, as opposed to the lazy indifference exhibited in so many other tiny Texas backwoods hamlets. Whether it's consciously reflecting the attitude of the townsfolk or not, the Horny Toad- which appears to be the only restaurant or bar in the area, also maintains a calm demeanor- at least on the Sunday that we visited. Saturday nights may be a different story at the Horny Toad. Certainly they've got the facilities for a backcountry good time. On the day when we went, though, it was a relaxed mix of bikers and Sunday tourists, all enjoying the gorgeous day in equanimity.

The Horny Toad has a full kitchen to cook up the usual country favorites, like nachos, chicken strips, and hamburgers. We can't say how meaningful their Best Burger Award is, though. It was certainly a good burger, but no more tasty than all the other delicious burgers that are cooked up in other Backcountry Hangouts. The only real problem was with the wait times, which were abnormally long even for food cooked to order. What was more impressive and pretty uncharacteristic this far out in the country was the white whale of country bars- a liquor license. Not only was there a good mix of beers, but they also have a full bar, able to mix up any cocktail one might desire, including a delicious Sunday morning Bloody Mary.

While the Horny Toad seems to attract a large complement of bikers, it's certainly not limited to that cohort. Along with the day-trippers out to see the scenery, there's also plenty of locals who stop in to eat, drink, and visit. The green painted building, with its old wood floors, outdoor patio, big screen TV's, and relaxed vibe makes for an atmosphere which can be enjoyed by all.

HUNT STORE

(830) 238-4410
www.thehuntstore.com
1634 Texas 39, Hunt, TX 78024

The Hunt Store in Hunt, Texas is a many-splendored thing. Serving as a focal point for this little river town, the Hunt Store contains just about anything you might need, including a bank, post office, grocery store, and restaurant.

While the outside isn't much to look at, the Hunt Store has been serving the area for many generations. You can get an idea of how old the building is by checking out some of the photos on the walls or just by going out to the patio area and looking at the outside of the building. The original structural walls can still be seen- old cedar posts arrayed vertically and filled in with limestone rocks and mortar.

Inside, the Hunt Store has a small modern bank, but still retains the old iron bars to, presumably, protect against bandits. Along with a well stocked drink cooler, the Hunt Store has a bustling kitchen which serves up all manner of sandwiches and barbecue, as well as something called a French Taco. Not to be confused with any sort of Continental cusine, a French Taco is something like a hamburger served in a tortilla and was prosaically named after a guy with the name of French, who first ordered it. The cozy dining room of the Hunt Store is ruggedly appointed with tables hewn from massive old trees and solid stumps for chairs, all lacquered to a fine polish. It's a bit like eating in at Disneyland, but without the singing bears.

Outside there's a large grassy patio, complete with picnic tables and firepits. On weekends, they have music- not limited to country pickers, but including jazz combos and the like. The only real drawback is that the Hunt Store only stays open til 9pm, which limits how much fun can be had there.

The Hunt Store isn't quite amazing enough, by itself, to be a true destination. It's certainly neat enough to warrant a visit though and, if you're staying in the area to enjoy the beautiful Guadalupe River, it's a good little place to while away some time. In the winter they always have a fire going in the hearth and it's a cozy and friendly place to hang out and have a drink, food and good cheer.

HYE MARKET

830-868-2300
hyemarket.com
10261 W. Highway 290, Hye, TX 78635

The Hye Market is a little place with big goals. While its ambition is to be small and quaint, it's going to be the best damn small-and-quaint market in Texas. Set hard by Highway 290 in between Johnson City and Fredericksburg, the Hye Market is positioned on one of the most popular tourist corridors in the state. Yet despite that prime location, the market and the town of Hye itself haven't been much more than a blink-and-you'll-miss-it kind of place for a long time. That's all changing now, though.

The Hye Market is located in the old Hye post office, which was built in 1904. It's a beautiful old gingerbread-trimmed building and is where LBJ mailed his first letter as a boy. The post office has now been converted into a high-end tasting room, featuring not just beers and wines, but also mixers, seasonings, vinegars, olive oils, and more. The ethos of the tasting room, and the adjacent restaurant, are to be sustainable, local, and have a really good story. Much of the food is made using local produce and meats. The menu changes, but features such items as locally sourced quail, lamb, and bison.

The owners of the Hye Market aren't content to sit on their laurels when it comes to making their town notable. In the future, they have plans to open more restaurants, B&B's, and a dancehall in Hye. Fortunately, they're not just looking to make a quick buck though. The same principles of sustainable, local, and a good story are being applied to all their plans for the rest of the town. They want to grow a place that is great to visit, but also great to live in. While the Hye Market is already a pretty good backcountry hangout by itself, we're looking forward to even more backcountry goodness in the Hye of the future.

JACKSON'S STORE

512-273-1131
Jacksonsstore.com
4312 W. FM 696, Lexington (Blue), TX 78947

Like so many tiny rural hamlets, Blue, Texas, has long since declined from being an established town with a school and shops and such, to a collection of houses within a close general proximity. Sitting between Elgin and Lexington on Highway 696, Blue at least still has Jackson's Store, a proper backcountry hangout, situated right next to the road.

Presumably named after the three Jackson brothers who settled the area in 1846, Jackson's Store is a classic country store. It's a ramshackle structure, surprisingly narrow, which houses a small grocery, a small bar, a small deli, and a small single pool table in the back room. They have all sorts of typical roadside diner type food, but they mostly serve cheeseburgers. Beer is sold out of a large igloo ice chest. The cooler of various chewing tobaccos, next to the cash register, is particularly fancy. What's not to like?

Jackson's Store is open every day of the week and they usually have, at least, Karoke every Saturday til 1am. Sometimes they even get some musicians to play on the open air patio out to the side. At Jackson's they're not trying to win any fancy accolades from Austin magazines for most "authentic" country experience. They're just doing a solid job serving the local populace and any tourists travelling the scenic highway.

Speaking of tourists- some of the folks travelling the road by Jackson's Store might be heading to Snow's BBQ in nearby Lexington. (Here follows a brief diatribe on barbecue: Snow's was voted #1 barbecue in Texas by Texas Monthly Magazine and they do a good job of keeping their product scarce by only opening on Saturdays from 8am until they run out. At least Franklin's in Austin has the decency to be open 6 days a week, even if he too subscribes to the annoying credo of artificial scarcity. It must be nice to have the financial means to only be open for half a day a week.) No matter your reason for being out near Blue, though, you owe it to yourself to stop for a cold drink at Jackson's and experience a genuine Texas country store.

JESTER KING BREWERY / STANLEYS
FARMHOUSE PIZZA

jesterkingbrewery.com
stanleysfarmhousepizza.com
13187 Fitzhugh Rd, Austin, TX 78736

The qualities that make for a good backcountry hangout can be pretty vague. There's a certain atmosphere that needs to be right. Isolation, picnic tables and beer definitely help too. The thing is- there are plenty of new places that try to create the old 'tin-shack-out-in-the-country' vibe, but which just don't feel legitimate. Somehow, Jester King gets it right. They've somehow managed to open a new place which already feels lived in and cool. I suppose it also doesn't hurt that part of the building is, indeed, an actual old tin building.

The Jester King Brewery is a working micro-brewery- making beer using really fancy-sounding things like "terroir", wild yeasts and "full attenuation"- whatever all that means. Whatever they're doing, though, is working. They make a ton of excellent beers- all of which can be enjoyed in either their tasting room or outside under the trees.

Thankfully, because Jester King focuses on beer, not food- right next door to Jester King is Stanley's Farmhouse Pizza. Their open-air wood-fired oven cooks up some delicious pizza that is the perfect complement to delicious beer. Although they're separate businesses, the close proximity of the two creates an unbeatable combination- providing everything one needs for a fantastic afternoon in the country.

Jester King, out on Fitzhugh Road, off 290 on the way to Dripping Springs, isn't exactly in the most isolated spot in Texas, but it's not bad. There's a lot of development out that way, but you wouldn't be able to tell from the rustic farm atmosphere of the brewery grounds. Outside of Jester King there are also more things to see and do nearby, including The Stunt Ranch, Argus Cidery, and the Magic's Theater & Museum. It's that kind of diverse weirdness that makes for good backwoods fun.

KENNEY STORE

(979) 865-2404
thekenneystore.com
811 Texas 497 Loop, Bellville, TX 77418

The Kenney Store is a country store with ambition. Primed and ready, it's got the tools and it's got the desire to be the next big thing in great country hangouts. Now, of course, normally, such ambition would be looked askance at. Trying too hard, in the country store game, is sometimes the first step down the road to mediocrity. The next thing you know, you're throwing plastic Hawaiian lei's over some deer antlers and serving beer in "collectable" cups. Fortunately, the owners of the Kenney Store, husband and wife duo Rita and Tony Krueger, appear far too savvy to fall into this trap. The Kenney Store that they're running is top-notch in all the ways that matter.

While the Krueger's have only owned the Kenney Store for a year or so, the store itself has been in existence since the late 1800's. In that time it's been variously a post office, general store, and beer joint. It's located in the tiny hamlet of Kenney, which is about 7 or 8 miles south of Brenham. The history of the place is evident all around, from the old building itself with its wood floors and pressed-tin siding, to the pictures on the wall showing various owners and patrons from decades past. It's not a dead history either. Former proprietors and old regulars still hang around the place, more than willing to share their memories of how it used to be.

The Kruegers, who themselves have deep roots in the community, have put a lot of time and effort into getting the place into shape to be something more than just an old beer joint. Without at all ruining the atmosphere of the place, they've put in a top of the line kitchen that serves up some of the best comfort food that we've ever tasted. And it's not just the kitchen itself- it's the fact that almost all of the items on the menu are made from scratch- down to the pickles and fried cheese sticks. Not only do they have fantastic versions of normal items like burgers and fries, but also backwoods delicacies like crawfish pies and fresh cooked pork cracklins. Oh, and don't forget the cold beer on ice- because a refrigerated beer just ain't the same.

With plenty of seating and a big dancefloor, the Kenney Store has all the room a body needs to enjoy himself on a weekend night. They've got bands booked every weekend, and there's a great jam session every Tuesday and Thursday evening. It might be a little bit of a hike to get there, but it's most definitely worth the trip, if not just for the music, then assuredly for the delicious food, great atmosphere, and friendly folks down in Kenney.

KNOT IN THE LOOP SALOON

(830) 685-3591
236 H and H Ranch Loop, Fredericksburg, TX 78624

The Knot in the Loop Saloon is not only one of the best named bars ever, but also one of the most cluttered. The pun name might derive from the fact that the bar is near where the scenic Willow City Loop is "tied" together with Highway 16, or maybe because it's "knot" directly on the Willow City Loop. The cluttered description comes from the amazing array of memorabilia and wacky tchotchkes scattered across the walls and ceilings of the place.

You could spend a couple of hours just looking at everything on display at the Knot in the Loop Saloon. It wouldn't be as worth visiting, though, if it wasn't also a good place to come have a beer and some good food. The Knot in the Loop serves up amazing burgers, as well as a few other items including fried catfish on certain nights.

Knot in the Loop was started about 10 years ago and has since grown into a great stop for motorcyclists and travelers on the Willow City Loop or Highway 16. What used to be a barn is now set back, all by its lonesome, just a few hundred yards from Highway 16. There's plenty of parking and one of the owners, Wayne or Robin, is likely to be tending bar. There's a jukebox, pool tables, and a nice porch to sit on out front , and, on nice days, some of the walls swing open to let the breeze blow through. It's worth it to do yourself a favor and take a break from the bluebonnets just long enough to grab a beer, a burger and a little shade at the Knot in the Loop.

LEON'S COUNTRY STORE

(512) 321-7346
4033 FM 535, Rockne, TX 78602

Leon's Country Store is mostly a bar. It might have once been a real country store and gas station, but these days the only thing they have for sale are some cold drinks- and that's pretty much okay with us. The funny thing about Leon's is that they have shelves full of old stuff like electrical fittings and hardware- but it's not actually for sale. It's like the store portion of the operation just sort of slowly wound down, leaving the bar side of things going, and everything else as a decrepit sort of country store museum. But, what a bar it is! If you like old-school country bars with none of the silly tourist-friendly claptrap, then this is the place for you.

Opened in the 1920's in Rockne (about half an hour southeast of Austin), Leon's is a rambling affair- wooden-floored and sagging. Like any good country bar, there aren't many windows and on a hot day, they've got the A/C on and plenty of cold beer. The treat here is the two pool tables, which only cost a quarter per game- although the beat-up condition of the tables probably wouldn't allow them to charge any more than they do.

While it's generally a beer joint- occasionally on weekends there are a few people who come and do some home cooking for whoever shows up. When we were there, they were preparing for a crawfish boil and believe me, they were cooking from scratch. No pre-peeled garlic or pre-cut lemon wedges for them.

When it comes down to it, Leon's is- according to one of the women doing some cooking- mostly just a place to drink. There are rarely any bands and they don't often serve food. As a place to drink, though, it's top-notch. Whether you're passing through on the way to Watterson Hall or just doing some exploring, it's a great place to cool off with a cold beer.

LONDON DANCEHALL

(325) 475-2921
17430 N Highway 377, London, Texas 76854
Hours: Thurs-Fri 5:00-12:00, Sat 6:00-1:00

The London Dance Hall has been around for a long time. So long, in fact, that they are in dispute with the far better known Greune Hall as to which dancehall is the oldest in Texas. The fact that the London Dance Hall is less well known is probably due to location. London is way out in the middle of the boondocks, on Highway 377 between Mason and Junction.

A tiny little hamlet of less than 200 people, London is a fascinating reminder of Texas past. This snapshot of Texas history includes a bygone gas station, a venerable country cafe, and several collapsing buildings in a state of picturesque decay. It's kind of like a town that time forgot, set in the wide Llano river valley and reachable only by traversing the beautiful and vast hill country landscape that surrounds it.

The dancehall and attached bar have been owned by the Ivey family for decades. In that time it appears to have been lovingly un-restored and left in a state of perpetual honky-tonk stasis. Its rather unattractive exterior and dark smoky interior attests to generations of redneck revelers untroubled by the burdens of effete urban sensibilities. Inside you'll find a nice little bar with a couple of pool tables and a fireplace. On Thursdays and Fridays the saloon area is open and provides a space for the locals to bring dishes for potluck dinners. During winter, there's a fire in the hearth and one could do a lot worse than to relax in the company of friends and watch the game. On Saturday nights they open up the dancehall and have a live band. Because it's pretty much the only thing going on in London- of course kids are welcome. While they only serve beer, setups are available and, if you're feeling hungry, they also have barbecue plates.

If you're really looking to get away from it all, there may be no better journey than to take a long drive through the verdant wildflowers of springtime and experience a night in Texas the way it used to be. Standing on the porch of the London Dance Hall, in the warm night air with some good country music wafting out the door, might be about as good as it gets.

LUCKENBACH

(830) 997-3224
www.luckenbachtexas.com
Luckenbach, TX

Luckenbach is the giant among Texas dancehalls. For name recognition alone, it is by far the most well known of all Texas dancehalls- partially because of the popularity of the 1977 song "Luckenbach, Texas (Back to the Basics of Love)" by Waylon Jennings and Willie Nelson. The popularity of Luckenbach is well deserved, as it plays host to live music every weekend, and the laid back vibe and relaxed atmosphere of the place, which includes not just the dancehall, but several other buildings and outdoor areas, is archetypal of how a Texas backcountry hangout should feel. Having said that, Luckenbach is hardly an undiscovered backwoods joint anymore. It has a gift shop for Pete's sake! The very popularity of the place can give it something of the feel of a tourist trap. Still, it wouldn't be popular without a reason. They serve up great music and the tiny town has a nice ambience that still takes you back to the good old days. There are plenty of great Texas country spots to visit, but Luckenbach is the only one that's required.

MORAVIA STORE

(979) 562-2217
www.themoraviastore.com
11501 Fm 957, Schulenburg, TX 78956

"957 Leads Right To The Door" is one of the slogans for the Moravia Store. South of Schulenburg on county road 957, the front door of the Moravia Store does indeed sit right next to the road, in the tiny backwoods hamlet of Moravia. Billing itself as one of the oldest country stores in Texas, the Moravia Store does indeed look pretty darn old. It's been in operation almost constantly since 1889- serving at various times as a general store, post-office, dancehall, saloon, and general meeting place for the community. These days the Moravia Store provides food, drink, and dancing in fine old country style.

The white wooden building has a noticeable lean when you walk in the front door and it's fortunate that Texas isn't earthquake prone. Inside you find a front room with tables, a great old wooden bar, and a whole lot of bric-a-brac on the walls and ceiling. They serve burgers, fries, and onion rings on Fridays and Saturdays and they have plenty of cold beer to wash it down.

In the back room there's a wooden dancefloor that's seen generations of Moravians waltz, two-step, polka, and chicken dance across it. It too is rich with memorabilia and junk, including many old license plates and a great wall featuring dozens of old beer company clocks.

To the side of the Moravia store there's an attached open air room with a pool table, another open air pavilion with picnic tables, and an incongruous red caboose which has tables in and around it as well. The men's bathroom is a sight, too. Covered in 80's pinup memorabilia, it will remind you why you once loved feathered hair and high heels.

The Moravia store in the daytime isn't the best time to visit, as the bartender can be a bit taciturn and the place is empty. While it's a fair hike from anywhere, it's definitely worth the drive to come out some evening and hang out with some good folks and listen to some good music.

OAKLEY'S LUMBERYARD BAR

(254) 896-5900
200 E Frederick St, Riesel, TX 76682

Oakley's Lumberyard Bar has a number of things to recommend it. There's the old lumberyard building that it's built inside. There's the fully stocked bar with not only beer and wine, but all the spirits as well. And then there are the waitresses. Oakley's specifically only hires cute young ladies, so...yeah.

Oakley's is set out in the tiny town of Riesel, about 10 or 15 miles outside of Waco, on the way to College Station and Houston. From the outside it has the look of a place that has been long abandoned. Step inside, though, and you'll enter the cool, dark environs of your classic Texas bar. You got your pool and darts and jukebox and big screen TV's. Out the back doors, you've got a sort of outdoors-ish space where they occasionally host crawfish boils or barbecues and where you can still see all the bays for the various pieces of lumber that used to be sold here too.

Whoever started Oakley's Lumberyard Bar knew what he was doing. Put a bar out in a tiny town on a busy highway and stock it with booze and women, and then every few weeks have a bikini or lingerie night. It's a recipe for success, even if it isn't remotely P.C. Oakley's isn't really a destination for the cultural traveler, roaming the backroads of Texas in search of our shared rustic heritage. Still, it's far from the worst place you could end up on a hot day.

OLD COUPLAND INN AND DANCEHALL

(512) 856-2777
www.oldcouplandinn.com
101 Hoxie St, Coupland, TX
Restaurant Hours: 5:30pm-10pm Friday and Saturday
Dancehall Hours: 7pm-12am Friday, 7pm-1am Saturday

The Old Coupland Inn and Dancehall has a really great porch out front. Raised above the street a bit, it looks out to the quiet streets of the small town of Coupland, northeast of Austin, and into the distance to the farms and fields of the countryside. It's a pleasant sensation to linger there for a while- the old-fashioned feeling of it serving as a mellow preamble to the good times to be had inside, for the Coupland has everything you need for a night out on the (small) town. There's a restaurant for getting your grub on, a dancehall for letting it all hang out, and an inn for crashing after a night of revelry.

The Old Coupland Restaurant serves up barbecue and steaks, and is open on Fridays and Saturdays. With an atmosphere like something out of a western movie, it's family style dining at its best. While they specialize in barbecue and steaks, they also have items like salmon, catfish, and shrimp. Don't forget to finish off with some cobbler for dessert .

Once you've stuffed yourself, it's time to enjoy the dancehall, which is directly next to the restaurant. While the dancehall is not one of those antique relics from the days of German pioneers, it's still a genuine honky-tonk. They have great musicians on Fridays and Saturdays and people come from far and wide to mix it up on the dance floor. The bar serves, not only beer, but mixed drinks as well.

Upstairs, the Old Coupland Inn has seven rooms available and is done in an 1800's brothel style. Think Victorian red velvet and polished oak- but not seedy or sordid. Each room has its own elegant style and décor to match it's name, such as the Scarlet Room, Bonnie Blue, or Bunkhouse. They also serve up a great country breakfast the next morning.

The Old Coupland Inn and Dancehall suffered for a few years under poor management. Quality slipped and the dancehall lost some of its charm. Fortunately, the original owners of the place, Barbara and Tim Worthy, have taken over again and refurbished and revamped the whole place. It's once again a fantastic weekend destination. It's only about 30 to 45 minutes from Austin, but it feels like a world from another time.

OSCAR STORE

(254) 983-2175
www.oscarstoretexas.com
8133 Oscar Spur, Temple, TX 76501

The vibe at the Oscar Store is one of casual informality. While kids entertain themselves out on the dancehall practicing their line-dancing moves, the parents can enjoy some rare grown up talk inside. The place is very busy and the waitresses are moving quickly, but the owner working the register seems in no hurry to ring up customers if he is chatting with regular locals. Since this is a place to go for a leisurely meal and entertainment, this is just fine. It adds to the charm, as it doesn't feel like a tourist place.

One assumes that the original Oscar Store, which burned down in 2005, had a bit more character than the current incarnation which, while nice, lacks some of the beloved quirks of a hundred year old building. In true country style, though, the furnishings aren't fancy and we trust that in a hundred years, the current Oscar Store will have the warm patina of well-worn age. (One of the things we liked the most were the ugly plastic rolling chairs that were at most tables. They were surprisingly comfortable and useful).

While the decor at the Oscar Store is somewhat utilitarian, with a few kitschy items on the walls here and there, the food is another story. The fried chicken was some of the best we've ever tried- at least as good as some renowned restaurants known for fried chicken- and the chicken fried steak was excellent too. We walked out stuffed, and with leftovers for another meal.

Outside the restaurant, Oscar Store has a great big indoor/outdoor dance floor and stage. Situated under the oak trees and next to an open meadow, the Oscar Store is a good place to listen to some live music on the weekends, have an adult beverage, let the kids dance and play themselves silly, and go home happy and satisfied.

PAIGE ICEHOUSE

512-253-6000
277 Old Hwy 20 East, Paige, TX 78659

The Paige Ice House is a newcomer to the Backcountry Hangouts scene- but it's got old roots. What was once an old gas station and garage, built in 1916, is now a nice little watering-hole in the tiny hamlet of Paige- a located about 45 minutes east of Austin on Hwy 290. Hanging from the rafters of the place, along with the various neon signs, are bunches of old engine gaskets. The bright and airy interior is nothing like an old dark and dirty garage though. The décor is colorful and eclectic and the wide front doors let in the breeze, making it a darn pleasant place to have a drink or three.

The Paige Ice House is owned and operated by Thomas and Norma Chalmers, who opened it in August of 2014, after having owned the location for years. Mr. Chalmers did all the work himself, including building what has to be the widest bar in Texas. The layout of the Ice House was done by Mrs. Chalmers according to the rules of Feng Shui, which also has to be a first for a Texas bar. Whatever she did- it's working.

The town of Paige isn't really all that far off the beaten path, being right alongside Highway 290 between Austin and Houston, but once you get a couple of blocks away from the highway, it feels pretty isolated. If you're looking for a nice place to stop and have a drink, and maybe shoot some pool, then the Paige Ice House is where it's at.

If you're looking for some dinner, you can also head down the road a short ways and go have a burger at the "old" Papa Woody's Icehouse, which is now the Paige Roadhouse. It's a nice place to get dinner, but if you want to relax and drink- go to the Paige Ice House.*

* While you're in Paige, stop by the famous Yarn-O-Rama just down the block from the Icehouse if you want to see a mind-boggling assortment of yarns and looms.

PONTOTOC VINEYARDS

(512) 658-0023
www.pontotocvineyard.com
17519 College Street, Pontotoc, Texas 76869

Normally one wouldn't include a vineyard and winery in a list of country stores and backwoods bars, but we found the Pontotoc Vineyard to be so enjoyable that we decided to include it here. Not only is it a fantastic place, but it shares some of the best qualities of the "hidden gems" that we're profiling, including being way out in the middle of nowhere and being almost unknown to the outside world.

If you're a Texas oenophile, then maybe you've heard of the Pontotoc Vineyard. If you're like most everyone else, you've never heard of Pontotoc, much less Pontotoc Vineyards. Pontotoc (pronounced Pawn-e-tock) is a tiny little hamlet located about 25 miles northwest of Llano on Highway 71. The town itself consists of a few scattered buildings and houses, along with a couple of interesting ruins. The scenery around the town, though, is as pretty as it gets in the Hill Country, with scenic views of the vast Llano River valley and dramatic granite outcroppings.

The Pontotoc Vineyard consists of an old stone building in the middle of town, along with a few acres of actual vineyard literally right out the back door of the place. The owners of the vineyard and the building have done a fantastic job of restoring the old building into a quite comfortable and lovely series of rustic tasting rooms. In the same building there's also a room which houses the winemaking equipment, stainless steel tanks, and the oak storage casks, as well as an old movie theater which is being converted into a small performance venue.

Right now, Pontotoc Vineyards themselves don't have a permanently open tasting room on site. Their tasting room is open by appointment. (The Money family, who own the vineyards and who have their hands full with small children, have their wines available at Wein Halle at the Community Hall on the main street in Fredericksburg.) What is open, however, is the tasting room for the excellent Dotson-Cervantes Wines.

Dotson-Cervantes is the label from the husband and wife team of Alphonse Dotson and Martha Cervantes. Alphonse is a former pro-football player who met Martha while living in Mexico. Somehow they made it out to Voca, Texas where they now run their own vineyard and winery. Go figure.

In Spring, when the weather is warm and the wildflowers are blooming, making a drive out to Pontotoc to relax with some delicious wines might be the best new day-trip in Texas.

REGENCY BRIDGE ④

The Regency Suspension Bridge, northwest of San Saba, is one of those places that most people have only read about. Situated off a remote backroad, it's about as out of the way as anywhere in central Texas. It's worth the trip though. Built in 1939 and restored in 1997, the Regency Bridge is a lovely span across the Colorado River, far below. Floored with wood planks, the bridge is still in use for vehicular traffic. Many people choose to drive over the bridge and then get out of their cars and walk on it as well. Perfectly safe, it's still probably best to drive over it first, before you see up close how thin the decking really is. It's also enjoyable to watch other cars drive over the bridge and see the bridge sway up and down.

The Regency Bridge is one of a very few suspension bridges left in Texas. Surprisingly, San Saba is relatively rich in bridges of the sort. There's another suspension bridge, now converted to foot traffic only, called the Beveridge Bridge, just north of town. Up until a few decades ago, there was also a vehicle suspension bridge over the Colorado by Bend.

Another notable point of interest near the bridge are the morteros in the rocks on the south side. On the top of the limestone cliffs, right next to the road, there are some holes ground into the stone by the native Americans-which were probably used to grind maize or acorns. Also, if you're visiting on a Saturday, be sure to visit the White Wolf Trading Company down the spur road on the north side of the bridge.

RILEY'S TAVERN

(512) 392-3132
www.rileystavern.com
8894 FM 1102, Hunter, Texas 78132

Barreling down I-35 between San Marcos and New Braunfels at 75mph, you'd be forgiven for missing the tiny hamlet of Hunter. Nestled under a grove of oak trees, the town of Hunter sits in happy obscurity, just a mile off the freeway, but a world away in temperament. The shady roads, rusted buildings, and the old railroad trestle hearken back to a time when Hunter was an important railroad stop for the cotton farmers and cattle ranchers of the area. Happily, there's one place that survives and thrives from that old era- Riley's Tavern.

The Riley's Tavern building has been in existence since the 1800's, and has been known as Riley's Tavern since 1933. James Riley- when he was just 17 year old- opened it back up after the end of Prohibition, and then ran the place for 58 years, until 1991. In fact, Riley's Tavern was awarded the very first beer license in Texas after Prohibition was repealed.

Riley's Tavern serves beer, wine, and mixed drinks. There is a long bar and plenty of seating inside, along with pool tables, a bandstand, popcorn machine, shuffleboard, and some pinball machines in various states of disrepair. Despite the low ceiling, the bar doesn't feel stuffy- as there are plenty of windows to let in the air and light. Out back in the Biergarten, Riley's Tavern has a laid back garden charm- along with a number of weekend bikers. There are plenty of patio tables to sit at, underneath the trees, as well as a horseshoe pit and another bandstand. None of this is to say that Riley's is pretty and clean. It's just got a nice wear to it, like a favorite t-shirt.

Riley's Tavern is open every day of the week from 1pm to midnight, except on Saturdays when they're open until 1am. They have live music almost every night, which can all be found on the online schedule.

SEFCIK HALL

(254) 985-2356
800 Seaton Rd., Temple, TX 76501

The Tom Sefcik Hall easily earns a place as one of the best backcountry hangouts in Texas. There's nothing not to like about this ninety year-old bar and dancehall. Set out among the fields east of Temple, the Sefcik Hall sits with a patina of casual country comfort, earned through countless days and nights filled with swinging music, cold beer, and good times.

Sefcik Hall is a white two-story wooden structure. On the bottom is a dark, but large, barroom. Old dark wood is the theme, from the bar to the tables. Behind the bar, the fantastic old neon Pearl Beer sign provides a soft glow. There's a couple of pool tables and a jukebox to the back, and the air-conditioned bar is just perfect after a hot day on the tractor. Upstairs is the dancehall. Reachable via the outside stairs, the dancehall is an excellent spot to try a bit of two-stepping, without being in an over-whelming city honky-tonk scene. The antique advertisements on the walls (original to the place- not purchased from some picker's warehouse) let you know just how old this place really is. While it's frequented mostly by an older crowd, the Sunday dances are a lot of fun and are a great place to kick it with some old-timers in a relaxed scene.

Sefcik Hall was built in 1923 by Tom Sefcik, and is still owned by his daughter, Alice Schulock. Speaking with a noticeable Texas-Czech accent, at around 90 years old, she's still as sharp as a tack and occasionally even heads upstairs to the dancehall to play saxaphone with the Polka bands. On the weekends, her son Kenny Schulock also helps out with the bar. They're both friendly as can be to both locals and outsiders.

Sefcik Hall is the type of place that other saloons want to be when they grow up. Year after year, it's provided solid service to thirsty farmers and ranchers in the Temple area. It's truly a one-of-a-kind place and not to be missed.

SHELBY STORE

(979) 836-8193
5072 Voelkel Rd, Fayetteville, TX 78940

The Shelby Store isn't necessarily what you'd call "inviting". The ramshackle grocery store/gas station/feed store has seen better days- as the peeling paint on the dilapidated structure can attest to. Still, no self-respecting country store would consider a new coat of paint or a facelift to be any sort of improvement. The somewhat intimidating nature of the place is instead provided by the characters who inhabit it. The group of guys sitting out front, drinking beer after a hard days work, might at first glance not seem very amicable to outsiders, but they readily shout back 'hello' and 'buenas dias' to a friendly overture. Inside, it's somewhat similar- with the cantankerous lady who owns the place giving off an air of suspicious cordiality.

It's well worth runing the gauntlet of unease, however, to visit the Shelby Store, in tiny Shelby, Texas. A classic country store, situated near the crossroads of remote Highways 1457 and 389 about halfway between Brenham and La Grange, the Shelby Store has been around for a long time and it looks to stay that way. The old wooden floors and low wooden ceilings are evidence of its long history in this old German community. Providing everything that the residents need, or at least needed in the past, the Shelby Store is haphazardly stocked with everything from cat food to Aqua Net, gasoline to deer corn. More importantly, the Shelby Store sells cold beer by the bottle- which you can enjoy inside or out.

Surprisingly, a while back, it appears that basketball star Yao Ming shot a commercial at the Shelby Store, and the owner of the store probably had enough of the limelight to last her for a while. The Shelby Store isn't looking to get on the map. The owner has no strong urge to attract camera toting tourists to see the colorful locals. The somewhat cool reception might be a defensive posture at the changing demographics of the area- what with rich city-folk moving in and buying up the farms and ranches of this beautiful area.

For all intents and purposes, they don't really care whether you show up or not. They don't serve the "best hamburgers" in Texas. They don't have ironic deer heads on the wall. They don't have any bands singing songs about its storied history and charms. All in all, it's not a place to bring all your friends to for the weekend- but it's a darn good place to stop and have a cold one during a long drive through the beautiful rolling hills of the surrounding countryside.

SISTERDALE SALOON

(830) 324-6767
1211 Sisterdale Rd, Sisterdale, TX 78006

The town of Sisterdale, despite being so tiny, has a lot to offer. A winery, a dancehall, an occasionally open barbecue joint, and the Sisterdale Saloon. Sitting right across the street from the special-occasion-only Sisterdale dancehall, the Sisterdale Saloon has all the classic elements of a great backcountry hangout. Old building? Check. Patio with picnic tables? Check. View overlooking farmland out back? Check. One hundred year old handcrafted bar? Check.

The Sisterdale Saloon sits directly on Sisterdale Road (Highway 1376), which runs between Luckenbach and Boerne. It's a popular drive, amidst the heart of bucolic Hill Country scenery, for cyclists- both motored and un-motored- as well as day-trippers from San Antonio. The Saloon makes for a great stop for travellers, as well as being a popular target for all the not-yet-ready-to-stop-partying, post-wedding guests from the dancehall across the street.

The Saloon building, constructed in 1954, has an old bar on one side. The actual bar itself was made in 1903 from Curly Pine and was brought over in a covered wagon. Through an open door by the bar, there's a nice big game-room with pool and shuffleboard. The real charm of the Saloon, though, is out the roll-up door where you'll find a large outdoor area with lots of shaded picnic tables. With its bandstand and views of the fields out back, the patio is a great place to hang out and listen to some good music, which they have live every Friday night.

The Sisterdale Saloon doesn't sell anything but beer and wine, but has setups available for the booze-hounds. There's also no food available, although they might occasionally throw something on the barbecue pit. Despite these minor drawbacks, if you're looking for a nice backcountry bar to have a beer, in a great little town, the Sisterdale Saloon has you covered.

SPECHT'S STORE

(830) 438-1888
www.spechts.com
112 Specht Rd, San Antonio, TX 78260

Specht's Store, Restaurant and Saloon is located outside of Bulverde, north of San Antonio. Specht's Store has been around since 1890 and amazingly, it still sits out by itself in the countryside- despite the creep of San Antonio suburbanization to the south. With its distinctive Texas flag painted on the roof, it's hard to miss... You're Welcome America!

In front there are picnic tables along the two-lane road where you can eat, drink, and watch the sunset. For those travelers that inherently need to "belly" up to something, inside one will find a bar and more tables for roadside socializing. Out back is a nice covered patio area with views of country staples, namely fields and cattle. On warm nights you can catch some live music on the patio and enjoy the ambience of a Hill Country evening.

Specht's serves up a variety of country comfort food, such as Chicken Fried Steak and Burgers, as well as the more surprising Sunday Eggs Benedict. Whether you are escaping the big city of San Antonio or just out for a country drive, stop by Specht's Store, pay homage to the giant Lone Star flag roof and enjoy!

STOCKTANK GENERAL STORE

(512) 778-6878
8950 Ranch Road 1869, Liberty Hill, TX 78642
Hours: Friday and Saturday noon to 9pm

The Stocktank General Store outside of Liberty Hill looks like it has been around since the late 1800's. The structure has the appearance of an old-time Mercantile, with its weathered wood, old-timey false front, and large front porch. Inside, you'll find an open and inviting space with a wood burning stove inside the front door.

Not a general store at all, Stocktank was actually built in 1986 and is open just on weekends, and particularly on Saturday nights. It's more of a music venue than anything else- with local musicians coming by to play on Saturday nights. Theresa and Pete Garner, the owners, are on hand to greet everyone and to man the little bar which only sells beer. The atmosphere is very welcoming, with good music and friendly folks in abundance. During winter, there's complimentary beans and cornbread to warm you up. In the summertime, the entertainment spreads outside and food is available from a food truck run by Theresa Garner herself. She serves up hamburgers, fried chicken, collared greens, etc.

Stocktank General Store is just about as nice and relaxing a place as a person could want. Located way out in the country, there's no hassle with parking or traffic. On the last Saturday of each month, you can bring your own instrument and jam with the various musicians who show up, or just sit on the porch with a beer and gaze over the meadows across the two-lane road out front.

TAYLOR CAFE

(512) 352-8475
101 N Main St, Taylor, TX 76574

We've tried to avoid including straight-up barbecue restaurants in this book. In Texas, there's already a surfeit of guidebooks and "experts" on the subject of barbecue and it's not in our interest to challenge any orthodoxy of this secular Texas religion. We couldn't help but want to write about the Taylor Cafe, though, because it has so many elements of a great Texas hangout. A lot of barbecue restaurants these days are massive affairs with big signs and huge followings. Not so the Taylor Cafe. Sitting hard by the railyard, in the shadow of an overpass, you could easily be forgiven in thinking that the Taylor Cafe is closed and abandoned. The little red corner restaurant sits on a tiny street next to some old buildings in downtown Taylor- looking like something out of an old Midwest rust belt city.

Opened in 1948 by Vencil Mares, fresh back from World War II, the Taylor Cafe has been serving up barbecue in Taylor lo these many years. Vencil himself has been holding court in the back of the cafe for that entire time. During that time he's seen the rise of barbecue culture in Texas and it's subsequent elevation to unimagined heights of devotion. Vencil himself has been noticed, even appearing in a Superbowl ad for Chevy pickups recently.

Still, Vencil and the Taylor Cafe don't put on airs. The place is remarkably free from anything which could be considered stylish or hip. It's most attractive feature is its sheer authenticity. There are tables on one side and two large counters in the middle. There's a jukebox and a pool table. The menu is written up on butcher paper and taped to the wall. If it weren't a real on-going operation, you'd think you were in a museum dedicated to mid-century Texas backwoods restaurant culture.

Legend has it that the two entrances and two counters are relics of segregation days and that the place is still self-segregated. We can't say one way or the other if this is the case. Certainly there didn't seem to be anything untoward when we were there, and one hopes that in this day and age we can all be brought together by the deliciousness of Texas barbecue.

TEJAS RODEO COMPANY

(830) 980-2226
www.tejasrodeo.com
401 Obst Road, Bulverde, TX 78163

The Tejas Rodeo Company is unlike anything we've seen before. It's something of a complete redneck package: a professional rodeo arena, dance hall, live music, restaurant, bar, mechanical bull (that's right, you heard me…) and more. Located out in the country west of Bulverde and north of San Antonio, Tejas Rodeo is a pretty new place. Typically, "new" and "touristy" do not make the list of "good ole' country places" , but Tejas Rodeo is the exception based on a great concept that really merges the old and new Texas spirits.

The Tejas Rodeo goes on every weekend from March until November. That's a real rodeo every weekend, folks- not just some dude ranch, show rodeo. The rodeo hosts real cowboys and real competition, with bull riding, roping, barrel racing, and more. There are also kid's events like the calf scramble and mutton busting. Immediately following every rodeo is a dance with live music on the dance floor conveniently located right next to the arena. There are outside bars which serve food and drinks, as well as a nice steakhouse- all located in one, convenient country mecca.

The Tejas Rodeo offers every weekend, what most Texas small towns do just once a year. It's like an all-inclusive, country getaway.

TRADINGHOUSE BAR AND GRILL

(254) 863-5251
4553 Lake Felton Pkwy, Waco, TX 76705

Driving up to the Tradinghouse Bar and Grill, one wouldn't be surprised to find Patrick Swayze out front, ejecting a few unruly drunks- Double-Deuce style. Standing at a crossroads, out east of Waco, the Tradinghouse has the look of an old-school roadhouse, and it's got everything needed to be one too. You got your big dirt parking lot, wide front porch, and a combination restaurant and saloon.

The restaurant at the Tradinghouse serves up your standard Texas country fare- think chicken fried steak, burgers, etc. On Fridays and Saturdays, the sign out front warns that there will be a 45 minute wait- so you know it's popular. Fortunately, the wait probably won't be too boring, since you've got a nice view of the countryside off the front porch and the bar next door is open and serving.

Out in back, through the bar, is a nice big patio with plenty of picnic tables. Off of the patio there's a good sized grassy area which has a bandstand big enough to welcome most any size band. It's a nice and relaxed environment and a person has just about all you need east of Waco- good food, good music, and good beer.

WALBURG GERMAN RESTAURANT AND BIERGARTEN

512-863-8440
www.walburgrestaurant.com
3777 FM 972, Walburg, TX 78673

For those of you who only go into the Hill Country for your explorations, it may come as a surprise to find that there exists a different but equally as authentic set of country locations east of I-35. Northeast of Austin, dotted between the farms and ranches in the rolling hills, are a variety of old establishments and communities that maintain the heritage of the Czech and German immigrants who settled there in the 1800's.

The Walburg German Restaurant and Biergarten in Walburg is as fine an example as can be had of the German heritage of Texas. The tiny town of Walburg sits atop the hills, looking mostly like it has for a hundred years, despite the encroachment a few miles west of the suburbs of Georgetown. Smack dab in the middle, at the intersection of FM 972 and FM 1105, the Walburg Restaurant serves up German food and entertainment like it's going out of style. The old building is filled with memorabilia celebrating the traditions of the early settlers. From Wednesday through Sunday, they serve up authentic German-Texas cuisine from Weinerschintzel to Chicken Fried Steak, and also serve up live music inside on weekends.

Out in the back of the restaurant, it gets even better. Situated behind the store, there is a large Biergarten, complete with a bandstand, tent, and picnic tables. Every weekend, during the warmer parts of the year, they have live music, food, and beer. It's like an Oktoberfest every weekend. Families and kids are welcome and encouraged, and there's never a cover charge. For kids who are not yet fans of polka music, there's also a well-stocked video arcade- but it's inside of an old barn-like building and doesn't detract from the ambience of the place.

Extra Credit:

Continuing on north through Walburg on FM 1105 the scenery becomes something reminiscent of an English countryside. The green fields and scattered houses stretch into the distance and a large double-spired church sits on a hill like an ancient country cathedral. Traveling on, you reach the tiny crossroads hamlet of Schwertner, containing some old stone buildings and the Schwertner Café, which sits in glorious unpretentiousness and serves up solid country fare with a smile.

If you take a right on FM 487 at Schwertner and continue driving east, you'll reach the town of Bartlett. Bartlett is a town which has seen more prosperous days. Its once fine neighborhoods now feature many old dilapidated houses and churches, many in a state of sad but beautiful decay. They are a testament to a time when this area was a far distance from anywhere else and the isolation from big box stores and malls necessitated a cohesiveness that no longer exists.

Driving through the pristine and empty downtown of Bartlett is a surreal experience. The main street features rows of buildings as well built and pretty as anything in Boerne or Fredericksburg- but now almost all vacant. Still, the future may be bright for Bartlett, as the growing population of Texas might one day rediscover this jewel-in-the-rough of a town.

WARING GENERAL STORE

(830) 995-4377
www.waringgeneralstore.com
544 Waring Welfare Rd, Waring, TX 78074
Hours: Monday thru Sunday 10am to 5pm,
Wednesday 6pm to 9pm

When you first see the Waring General Store, you just know you're going to have a good time. After a pleasant drive along country back roads, the tiny town of Waring sits as it has for a hundred years in the midst of the farms and ranches northwest of Boerne. The Waring General Store nowadays isn't really a store at all, but a restaurant and dancehall.

Built in what used to be an old gas station and then later a tractor dealership, the Waring General Store now has a large indoor eating area and dancehall, as well as an outside patio and stage. The vibe both inside and out is one of kitchy rustic nostalgia, with plenty of rusty signs, Texas memorabilia, picnic tables, etc.

The menu for the grill, which is open every day from 10am to 5pm, is classic American, with giant, delicious hamburgers. Of course- beer, wine, and sodas are available. The real treat at the Waring General Store, however, is steak night. Every Wednesday night, one can get a great steak dinner as well as listen to live music on the stage. What else do you need? The Waring General Store has everything necessary for a great hangout.

WATTERSON HALL

(512) 304-5860
1179 Watterson Rd, Red Rock, Texas, 78662

Like a lot of Texas dancehalls, from the outside Watterson Hall doesn't look very promising. A tin-roofed, tin-sided structure on a backroad in the middle of nowhere, it's front windows blocked with what looks like insulation, the utilitarian-looking Watterson Hall sets a pretty low bar for dancehall design enthusiasts. Step inside, though, and you'll find many of the classic dancehall touches- and a few unusual ones as well. In addition to the open rafters, the wooden dancefloor, and the wooden chairs and tables to the sides- there's a nice chandalier in the middle of the hall, and a big Texas star painted in the middle of the dancefloor.

Watterson Hall was opened in 1952 by the father of Leroy Wilhelm, and is still run by Leroy and his wife. They have dances with live bands almost every Saturday night and are also often booked for weddings of every type. The other big draw of Watterson Hall is the hamburgers, which are very tasty and nicely priced. Regular hamburgers start at $2.75 and go up from there all the way to a triple-meat burger for a reasonable $5.00. You can wash them down with a very affordable $2.00 beer. As if that's not cheap enough- they have a happy hour from 5:30-7 on Saturday evenings before the dance gets started.

Perhaps most famous for being the setting of the "dancehall" scene from the Sandra Bullock film 'Hope Floats', Watterson Hall is set in isolation amidst the fields and farms about 20 minutes south of Bastrop. That isolation is precisely what makes this place so cool. A warm saturday night, with a cold beer and a swingin' band doesn't get any better than it does out here in the middle of nowhere.

WHITE WOLF TRADING POST

325-938-5224
Facebook.com/regencyfestival

In the new cosmopolitan Texas, with its wine tasting rooms and bed and breakfasts, it's getting harder to find that outlaw hippie spirit which emerged in the early 1970's with Willie and Waylon and Austin's Armadillo World Headquarters. With the explosive growth of Texas cities and suburbs and the (welcome) influx of out-of-staters, it's been a challenge not to destroy the very things we all love about Texas.

Fortunately, there still exists a place which retains that backroad easy-going hippie-redneck non-conformist charm. The White Wolf Trading Post, on the banks of the Colorado River next to the Regency Bridge, is just about as close as you can get to time-travelling back to something like Luckenbach, before it got discovered. Owned and operated by Sue and Alton Watson, the White Wolf Trading Post is variously a country store, dancehall, and outdoor lounge- in assorted stages of disrepair. For years, Sue and Alton ran the store, which catered to visitors and campers. With the closing of the nearby campground, the store didn't have enough business to stay open regularly. Still, the Watsons welcome visitors on Saturdays who might want to stop by and drink a few beers. If you bring a guitar and can pick a few songs- well...that's even better.

Make no mistake, the White Wolf Trading Post ain't pretty. Like any authentic backwoods hangout, there's junk scattered all around, including a rusting school bus out back. Still, sitting outside with a cold beer, listening to Alton and Sue play a country song on the guitar, you'll realize that this is as good and as real as it gets. The Watsons are just about as friendly as can be, and Alton comes straight out of central casting with his gravelly voice and long scraggly beard. Even better, there's often a friend or two who will stop by and join in the conversation and music-making- which is as unhurried and relaxed as befits this out of the way locale.

The White Wolf Trading Post isn't open all the time and it's probably best to call and see if someone's going to be around before you come out. The best time of all to visit, though, might be during the one and only official event that is held there- the 'There's Something In The Water Music Festival'. Held on or around Easter weekend, the festival brings together musicians from all over to play and hang out. Ostensibly held in a beat up old building next door, the weekend crowd of a few hundred is just as likely to stay up late around the fire passing a bottle and trading off playing songs.

So, if you're finding the Texas you're in to be too fast-paced and crowded, think about taking a long country drive out to the White Wolf Trading Post where life is still slow and easy. To get there- from San Saba head north on Highway 16 for about a mile until you see the sign for Regency Bridge. Take a left and travel on County Road 500 for about 14 miles. At the sign for Regency Bridge, turn right and drive for a half mile or so and cross the bridge. The entrance to White Wolf Trading Post is on the right hand side, immediately past the bridge. The store is through the gate and down the road a couple of hundred yards.

WHIZZERVILLE HALL/R&G BAR-B-QUE

(512) 398- 4601
Whizzervillehall.com
6320 FM 713, McMahan, TX 78616
Open Weds-Sun 11am-9pm

Whizzerville Hall has to be one of the best named hangouts we've come across. Named after the old town name (now called McMahan), Whizzerville Hall is one of only a few old buildings in this tiny hamlet about 10 miles east of Lockhart at the intersection of Farm Roads 713 & 86. Formerly a general store, the Whizzerville Hall building is 104 years old, but has been kept in good condition. It's wood floors and big bay windows have served generations of residents, back to the days when McMahan was a bustling town of 250 citizens. The whole town itself was bought by the Douple family a few years ago, who opened the Whizzerville Hall in its current incarnation.

Whizzerville Hall doesn't serve up your usual Texas backcountry staples, like barbeque and hamburgers, instead, they create some of the best pizza around, with names like "The Longhorn" and "The Cotton Eyed Joe". In addition to pizza, they also have po' boy sandwiches, wings and ice cream, and of course a good selection of flavored iced teas and beer.

In the past few years, Whizzerville Hall has had regular live music on weekends, both inside and outside on the back patio. Right now, they're putting up an addition to the Hall, which will expand the space available- which means that they won't have music for a while, but it's sure to be back sometime.

Directly across the road from Whizzerville Hall is R&G Bar-B-Que. While Whizzerville might be the classier joint in town, R&G's isn't a slouch when it comes to being a good backcountry hangout. Also housed in an ancient building, R&G's serves up delicious barbeque and burgers in a dining room that can easily be described as "eclectic"- with the old store decorated in a strange thrift-store sort of manner. R&G's is run by famed cooker Roy Jeffrey- who's been smoking barbeque for over a half century in places like City Market of Luling and Luling City Market in Houston. He's known for his brisket and sausage, as well as his legendary mustard sauce. Like Whizzerville, R.G.'s also serves beer- but they sell it in cans, while across the street, Whizzerville sells only bottles. Vive la difference!

All this just goes to show that there's an option for almost everyone in this tiny town- if you can find it.

THE WILLOW CITY LOOP

If you're visiting the Knot in the Loop Bar or Harry's on the Loop, then you're very likely to be heading for the Willow City Loop. If you're not familiar with the Willow City Loop, then you're in for a treat. The Loop is a roughly 20-mile stretch of beautiful Texas backroad, which wends it's way through some amazing Hill Country scenery. The Loop is most popular in springtime, when the Bluebonnets and Indian Paintbrush are in bloom, although it's a wonderful drive almost any time of year. The road meanders from cedar covered limestone uplands down into oak filled, steep sided, granite canyons. The drive down into the valleys encompasses the transition from the monoculture limestone of much of central Texas into the mineral richness of the Llano uplift. It's full of stunning vistas and bucolic scenery.

Really nothing more than a small county road, the Willow City Loop can get very crowded during flower season- even on weekdays. Remember to respect the land-owners who have to put up with heavy traffic, and don't trespass. Also make sure and check for snakes before setting your kids down on the ground for those family photos in the bluebonnets. (Nothing ruins a family outing faster than a rattlesnake bite)

The Loop essentially starts and stops on Highway 16, between Fredericksburg and Llano. One can choose either direction to travel on the road. From Fredericksburg, go 12 miles north on Highway 16, then right on FM 1323. Go about two miles to Willow City; the Loop begins there. One can also start at the other end of the road, which is about 8 miles past FM 1323 on Highway 16, and which is marked with a sign. In either case, make sure and stop at Harry's or Knot in the Loop afterwards to have a cold drink and congratulate yourself for being able to experience such a beautiful little part of planet Earth.

Wait! There's more!

Following are a few advertisements from some friends of mine. Now- I hate over-zealous capitalism as much as the next bearded-socialist, but sometimes you've just got to get the word out about a good deal. My goal is to let you all know about some cool enterprises near where I live, and not just lard up this book with a bunch of ads for tire shops and exterminators. Hopefully, this little bit of commercialism isn't too crass and I really hope you'll patronize these places on your next backcountry journey. If I didn't believe they were worth checking out, I wouldn't have put them in my book.

-RH

LLANO RIVER REGION ADVENTURES

The Author Says:

I grew up around the Llano River and it is, without a doubt, one of the prettiest and most unspoiled rivers in Texas. Most of my time on the river has been spent between Castell and Kingland- and it's pretty great. Up by Mason, where Tony Plutino, the owner of Llano River Region Adventures lives, though, it's even better. You get the full experience of a river that hasn't much changed since before man arrived. The water is clear, the banks are undeveloped, the magnificent rocks are un-graffitied, and, if you camp, the stars are unspoiled by city lights. There are also lots of other things to do up there, besides floating on the river, and Tony can set you up with just about any sort of activity you might desire, from seeing Native-American pictographs to touring some Hill Country wineries. So, go get Tony on the horn and set yourself up for a little adventure this weekend.

LOST ROCKY MOUNTAIN RANCH

The Author Says:

I am lucky enough to live right nearby the Lost Rocky Mountain Ranch here in Llano. Now, when I was growing up, we had to go to a zoo to see animals from darkest Africa and Asia. Nowadays, I just have to look out my window to see critters like Scimitar Horned Oryx, Wildebeest, Fallow Deer, Blackbuck Antelope, Gemsbok, Sika, Red Deer and more. I have to say, it's pretty cool to see these animals living here, in a spot where they can be grown, protected, and managed in a way that insures their survival as a species.

Over the past few years, I've gotten to know Steve, the owner of the Lost Rocky Mountain Ranch. My Dad and I have done some bulldozing and tractor work for him and he's been kind enough to let us drive around the ranch. Let me tell you- it's pretty amazing. I hadn't realized how stunning the scenery could be back in these canyons. Steve has an incredible place- and he doesn't scrimp when it comes to the lodging either. If you want a top notch experience and want to bag that trophy buck while living in style, you owe it to yourself to check 'em out. Give me a holler too, while you're here.

PHOENIX NEST GUEST HOUSES

From a country setting on a quiet ranch to a quaint home in the city of Llano, Phoenix Nest Guest Houses offers something for everyone.

Lony and Joan Reed, Proprietors
14273 South State Hwy 16
Llano, Texas 78643
325-247-2720 or 325-248-4376
phoenixnestguesthouses@gmail.com
www.phoenixnest.com

Mention this book and get 10% off any stay of 2 or more nights

The Author Says:

If there are any Guest House moguls in Llano County, they've got to be Lony and Joan Reed of the Phoenix Nest Guest Houses. Their empire consists of 6 different houses ranging from spacious in-town cottages to private country getaways. You can be sure that whatever you're looking for, they'll have an option for you- when you're ready to experience the charms of small-town Llano.

I've known Joan Reed since I was a wee tyke. Back when she was Joan Myers, she and my mother were good friends and I have many fond memories of hanging out with the Myers family. Her late husband, Jim, was in the Army Reserves with my Dad, as well as having a friendly business rivalry with their respective beer distributorships- Jim of Lone Star and my Pa with Anheuser-Busch.

Since moving back to Texas, I've had the opportunity to reconnect with Joan and to meet her new husband, Lony. Joan is never without a big smile and she and Lony bring their country friendliness to all aspects of their operation. So, the next time you're here in the Hill Country, skip the Super 8 and make your vacation more memorable by staying at one of the Phoenix Nest Guest Houses.

BARBARA HOUSTON REAL ESTATE

The Author Says:

What sort of son would I be if I didn't include my own Mother's business in here? Fortunately, she's a great real estate agent and broker, on top of being a great Mom, so I didn't have to think too long about whether to include her or not.

One of my Mom's favorite things to do is to drive around various neighborhoods, looking at houses. Now, you can imagine how much fun this was for me and my brothers when we were kids.   I'm pretty sure the complaining began not more than two to three minutes into such drives. Despite us boys, though, she has a deep knowledge of many, if not most, of the neighborhoods in Austin. Combine that with her long experience in Interior Design and she's got pretty much all the skills you'll need for buying or selling a home. Trust me, she's good. After all, look how well I turned out!

ABOUT THE AUTHORS

Rich Houston

Part-time rancher, part-time slacker, Rich grew up on a ranch in Llano, Texas. His primary goal upon reaching the age of majority was to leave Texas as fast as he could. After 20 years away seeing the world, he was finally ready to come back and appreciate all that Texas has to offer. He now lives on the ranch again, where he spends most of his time devising ludicrous business schemes and exasperating his father.

Heather Kuhn

Yet another carpet-bagging east-coast transplant, Heather Kuhn has proven herself adaptable to the blast-furnace summertime culture of Texas. Excelling at river swimming, rope swinging, back-road driving, and porch sitting, Heather has, with this book, put herself at the forefront of redneck haute culture. When she's not working 18 hours a day, she enjoys reading, happy hour, tending to goats, gardening, cooking, and trying as many new foods as possible.

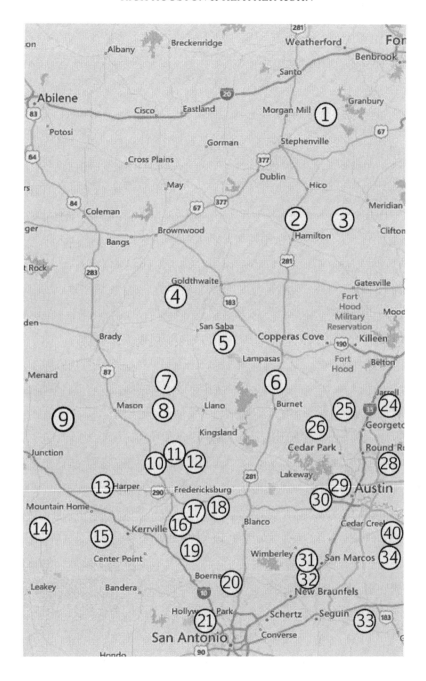

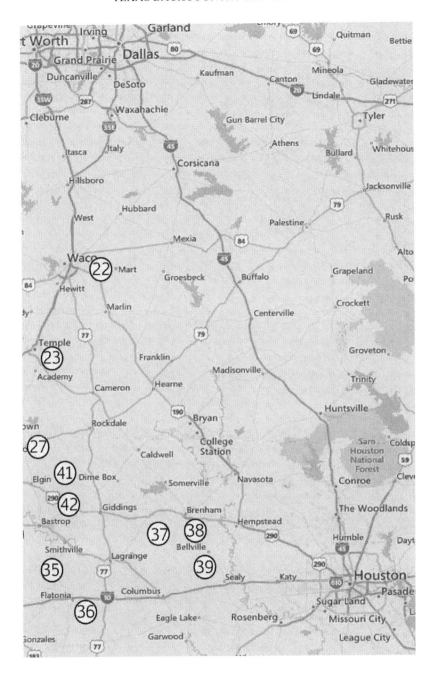

Made in the USA
San Bernardino, CA
27 October 2015